THE TRAGIC CASE OF LIU XIAOBO

HEARING

BEFORE THE

SUBCOMMITTEE ON AFRICA, GLOBAL HEALTH, GLOBAL HUMAN RIGHTS, AND INTERNATIONAL ORGANIZATIONS

OF THE

COMMITTEE ON FOREIGN AFFAIRS
HOUSE OF REPRESENTATIVES

ONE HUNDRED FIFTEENTH CONGRESS

FIRST SESSION

JULY 14, 2017

Serial No. 115–45

Printed for the use of the Committee on Foreign Affairs

Available via the World Wide Web: http://www.foreignaffairs.house.gov/ or
http://www.gpo.gov/fdsys/

U.S. GOVERNMENT PUBLISHING OFFICE

26–226PDF   WASHINGTON : 2017

For sale by the Superintendent of Documents, U.S. Government Publishing Office
Internet: bookstore.gpo.gov   Phone: toll free (866) 512–1800; DC area (202) 512–1800
Fax: (202) 512–2104   Mail: Stop IDCC, Washington, DC 20402–0001

CONTENTS

THE TRAGIC CASE OF LIU XIAOBO

<hr>

FRIDAY, JULY 14, 2017

HOUSE OF REPRESENTATIVES,
SUBCOMMITTEE ON AFRICA, GLOBAL HEALTH,
GLOBAL HUMAN RIGHTS, AND INTERNATIONAL ORGANIZATIONS,
COMMITTEE ON FOREIGN AFFAIRS,
Washington, DC.

The subcommittee met, pursuant to notice, at 10:00 a.m., in room 2172, Rayburn House Office Building, Hon. Christopher H. Smith (chairman of the subcommittee) presiding.

Mr. SMITH. The subcommittee will come to order, and good morning to everyone.

Liu Xiaobo's premature death was a jarring shock to everyone who admired this champion of freedom and democracy. We mourn his loss because it is a tragic loss for his wife, family, and friends, and a catastrophic loss for China and really the entire world.

We owe Liu Xiaobo a debt of gratitude because he demonstrated that the noble idea of democracy and due process, liberty, and the rule of law are not foreign ideas to China. They are universal principles that beat strongly in the hearts of people everywhere, from New Jersey to California, to the Nineveh Plain, to Iraq, from Poland to Peru, from Burma to Beijing.

We owe Liu Xiaobo a debt of gratitude because he reminded us that the desire for democracy and human rights is shared by everyone because each person is endowed by the Creator with inalienable rights.

The Chinese Communist Party has tried to curtail his ideas, they call them dangerous and subversive, and they seek to silence, censor, and repress them. Yet they live on in the hearts of untold millions of Chinese people.

With Liu Xiaobo's death we also reminded of the words of Dr. Martin Luther King who said, "Injustice anywhere is a threat to justice everywhere." We should all agree that what was done to Liu Xiaobo and his wife Xia was a grave injustice.

Liu Xiaobo's imprisonment in 2009 became a death sentence. The blame for this should lie squarely on the Chinese Government, and for his death, they alone, should be held accountable. Liu Xiaobo was the first Nobel Peace Prize winner to die in state custody since Carl von Ossietzky died after being held in a Nazi concentration camp.

Two days ago, we heard the Chinese Government complaining that it was stabbed in the back by those expecting it to deal quickly with its client state of North Korea. How shameful it is to play the victim card while the victim of their own repression lay dying.

No nation should be judged entirely by crimes of the past, but this crime, the death and silencing of Liu Xiaobo, should follow the Chinese Communist Party like an unwashable permanent stain. We must never forget Liu Xiaobo's enduring contributions, whether during the Tiananmen massacre where he helped save the lives of many students, or with Charter 08, the treatise urging political and legal reforms in China based on constitutional principles.

We must not forget Liu Xiaobo. We must advance and preserve his legacy and repeatedly confront the Chinese Communist Party with his ideas and his memory. In this time of need, we must signal the Congress' unanimous support for Liu Xiaobo's family, his wife Xia, and all those bravely standing up for human rights and liberty in China.

I was invited by Liu Xiaobo's family to attend the 2010 Nobel Peace Prize ceremony. It was a moving ceremony. The now famous empty chair, and we have a photograph of that over on my right, speaks volumes of the Chinese Communist Party's abiding fear that human rights and democracy will undermine its power.

I will always remember the words of Liu Xiaobo's speech that day—of course not given in Oslo—about the importance of pressing for human rights. "Freedom of expression," he said, "is the foundation of human rights, the source of humanity, and the mother of truth. To strangle freedom of speech is to trample on human rights, stifle humanity, and suppress truth."

He also expressed his hopes for China's future. He said, "I firmly believe that China's political progress will not stop. And I, Liu Xiaobo, filled with optimism, look forward to the advent of a future free China. For there is no force that can put an end to the human quest for freedom, and China will be in the end will become a nation ruled by law where human rights reign supreme."

Liu Xiaobo would, sadly, never see a free China. Chinese authorities have gone to great lengths to stifle his ideas and those who followed him. In recent years, the government of President Xi Jinping has engaged in an extraordinary assault on the rule of law, human rights, ethnic minority groups, and civil society. As China's economic and military power grows, more and more countries will be afraid to raise subjects that the Chinese Communist Party wants to make taboo.

The U.S. stands alone, inadequate as its efforts are at times, in its willingness to keep on raising human rights issues that need to be raised. The U.S. cannot lightly shrug off the mantle of being democracy's defender no matter how heavy that mantle may become. It is tempting to be pessimistic about China's future and the future of U.S.-China relations. But I am not pessimistic, and taking a cue from Liu Xiaobo, none of us should be. Constant repression has not dimmed the desire of the Chinese people for freedom and reform, and, of course, that is attributed to the great work of Liu Xiaobo.

Nevertheless, the U.S. cannot be morally neutral or silent in the face of the Chinese Government's repression of fundamental freedoms. Human rights are not a secondary interest, but one critically linked to all issues in China, including U.S. economic and security interests.

The U.S. must not shy away from meeting with China's other Nobel Laureate, the Dalai Lama, or other dissidents. We must use congressionally authorized sanctions to hold Chinese officials accountable for torture and gross abuses, including those proscribed in the International Religious Freedom Act and of course, the Global Magnitsky Act.

We must connect Internet and press freedoms as both economic and human rights priorities. And we must demand repeatedly and clearly that unconditional release of political prisoners is in the interest of a better U.S.-China relationship.

I believe that someday China will be free, someday the people of China will be able to enjoy all of their God-given rights, and a nation of free Chinese women and men will honor and celebrate Liu Xiaobo as a hero. He will be honored along with others like him who have sacrificed so much and for so long for freedom.

I yield to my distinguished ranking member, Karen Bass.

Ms. BASS. I want to thank our witnesses for joining us today. I extend my condolences to Liu Xiaobo's family and friends on his recent passing.

Chairman Smith, you have long been a champion, as demonstrated by your actions over the years and today.

The loss of Liu Xiaobo has once again brought attention to the issues of human rights in China. Tragically, his imprisonment and passing is a reminder of the importance of monitoring the treatment of those who have been imprisoned or who have lost their lives fighting for freedom, freedoms like the freedom of religion, speech, press, and the right of people to peacefully assemble, as well as the often-implied freedom of association.

Central to those freedoms is the freedom to petition the government for a redress of grievances. Liu Xiaobo spent the final months of his life appealing to the Chinese Government to allow him to leave China to receive cancer treatment, and even in his final request he was denied.

He could have lived a quiet life as an academic, a scholar, a writer, but instead he decided to challenge the status quo and actively engage in efforts for democratic reform. He leaves behind the embers of democratic principles that will be fanned by generations to come.

I yield.

Mr. SMITH. I thank my good friend for her comments.

I would like to now recognize our very distinguished panel, beginning with Yang Jianli, who was born in Shandong Province in northern China and graduated from college at the age of 19. A rising star in the Chinese Communist Party, Yang Jianli quickly became disenchanted by the corruption and duplicity he witnessed in the Communist system.

He left China to pursue a career in mathematics at UC Berkeley. In 1989, at the age of 26, his fellow graduate students at Berkeley elected him to go back to Beijing in support of their counterparts in China who were demonstrating for democracy in Tiananmen Square. After escaping the gruesome massacre, he dedicated his entire life in promoting a peaceful democratization.

He received his Ph.D. in mathematics from UC Berkeley. But of significance, when he returned to China in 2002 he was put in prison for 5 years. Upon his release he founded Initiatives for China. So he knows the inside of a gulag.

And we thank him for being here, especially with the loss of his brother-in-law. And he will be going to that funeral right after here. He wanted to be here so badly.

We will then hear from Jared Genser, the founder of Freedom Now and managing director of Perseus Strategies. Previously, Jared was a partner in government affairs at DLA Piper. He is a visiting fellow at the National Endowment for Democracy. His human rights clients have included Vaclav Havel, Aung San Suu Kyi, Liu Xiaobo, Desmond Tutu, Elie Wiesel.

He holds a B.S. From Cornell and a master's in public policy from the John F. Kennedy School of Government at Harvard. He got his J.D. cum laude from the University of Michigan Law School.

He is an author of "The U.N. Working Group on Arbitrary Detention: Commentary and Guide to Practice," and he is a co-editor of "The Responsibility to Protect: The Promise of Stopping Mass Atrocities in Our Times."

And I want to thank him for his tenacious leadership for Liu Xiaobo and other wonderful and leading dissidents around the world.

Then we will hear from Perry Link, who is professor emeritus of East Asian studies at Princeton University and chair for Teaching Across Disciplines at the University of California at Riverside. He has published widely on modern Chinese language, literature, and popular thought. As a member of the Princeton China Initiative, Human Rights Watch Asia, and other groups that support human rights, he has authored many, many books, and he has testified here in the past as well.

I would like to go to Dr. Yang.

STATEMENT OF YANG JIANLI, PH.D., PRESIDENT, INITIATIVES FOR CHINA

Mr. YANG. Chairman Smith and Ranking Member, I had a sleepless night. At this grievous moment I would like to thank you for holding this critical hearing. It is critical for us to discuss how we can still lend a helping hand to assist Liu Xiaobo and his family and how we can fight to honor the legacy of his courage and sacrifice.

Liu Xiaobo's tragedy represents the tragedies of many human rights activists in China, but it is also unique in its own way. In all of the Nobel Peace Prize history there have only been three jailed laureates, but among them Liu Xiaobo is the most tragic one.

Liu Xiaobo had been held incommunicado since December 2008 until he became terminally ill and was eventually allowed a visit by a German doctor and an American doctor after the pleas to Xi Jinping from both President Trump and German Chancellor Merkel.

During his entire imprisonment he was not allowed even to talk about any current events with his wife Liu Xia during her visits, nor the persecutions Liu Xia and her family suffered. Even on his deathbed he had no freedom to leave his last words. Now that he is gone, the world will never know.

Liu Xiaobo's cancer was diagnosed on May 23 during an emergency hospital visit because of internal bleeding. And since then he had been hospitalized in the First Hospital of China Medical University in Shenyang, Liaoning Province. However, the news of his late stage cancer was not leaked out until late June.

During this time his tumor enlarged from 5 to 6 cm to 11 to 12 cm. It is reported that Liu Xiaobo had two CT tests last year. How can two tests—two tests—fail to reveal Liu Xiaobo's fairly large liver cancer tumors? Many, including myself, suspect that the Chinese officials intentionally concealed this information. This is why they have been withholding his medical records. These records are classified as a top state secret.

I strongly believe that the Chinese regime deliberately chose not to treat Liu Xiaobo's cancer earlier. As early as 2010, Liu Xiaobo was suspected of suffering from hepatitis B. His lawyers had been petitioning the government to grant him medical parole. But the Chinese authorities never allowed him proper diagnosis and treatment.

In China it is not doctors, but the party officials to decide whether to grant medical parole. In other words, medical parole in China is a political, not a medical decision.

In Liu Xiaobo's case, it was up to China's top leaders to decide. The denial of medical care led to Liu Xiaobo's advanced liver cancer and at its core was a disguised death sentence.

When Liu Xiaobo's worsening condition became public, human rights activists, 150 Nobel laureates, and world leaders called for Liu Xiaobo's immediate release and medical treatment overseas. Liu Xiaobo himself also expressed his wish to seek medical treatment abroad and to die in a free place.

Unfortunately, the Chinese regime carelessly disregarded these requests. After persecuting him for so many years, the regime still did not even hesitate to crush his final wish.

I believe the reason that the Chinese regime denied Liu Xiaobo's wish and the world's appeal to allow him medical treatment abroad and to die in a free place is that it fears that the truth of its ruthless persecution will come to light. The world media would focus on Liu Xiaobo and the regime's lies would be exposed More and more people in China would see the true nature of this one-party state. The government would lose control.

No doubt, the Chinese Communist regime is responsible for Liu Xiaobo's death. However, the world's democracies' appeasement policy toward China's human rights abuses has made them accomplices of Liu Xiaobo's slow murder.

If the world continues to acquiesce to China's aggression against its own people, engaging it without any moral clarity, Liu Xiaobo's tragedy will repeat.

Mr. Chairman, the U.S. can and should do more to help Liu Xiaobo and his family. We should urge the Trump administration to make it a high priority to urge China to grant Liu Xia full control over any funeral arrangements for her late husband and to help Liu Xia to leave China for a country of her choosing.

The U.S. should implement country-specific and tougher sanctions against those personally responsible for Liu Xiaobo's death. The U.S. should use the Global Magnitsky Act as a tool to sanction them, banning them from travelling in the U.S., and freezing their assets in this country, and also encourage its allies to do the same. It should also consider trade sanctions.

In addition, the U.S. can honor Liu Xiaobo's life and legacy by passing legislation to permanently rename the street in front of China's Embassy in Washington, DC, as Liu Xiaobo Plaza.

To fight for the ideals of human rights and democracy Liu Xiaobo give up his career, he gave up his freedom, and now he has given up his life. But we cannot give up on him. We have to seek justice for his death at the hands of China's regime, and we have to preserve the legacy of Liu Xiaobo's struggle for a democratic, free China.

Thank you.

[The prepared statement of Mr. Yang follows:]

Written Materials Submitted to the House Foreign Affairs Subcommittee on Africa, Global Health, Global Human Rights, and International Organizations for Its Hearing on "The Tragic Case of Liu Xiaobo," July 14, 2017

Yang Jianli
Initiatives for China/Citizen Power

I.   Opening Remarks

Chairman Smith and Ranking Members of the Subcommittee, at this grievous moment, I would like to thank you for holding this critical hearing which focuses on the only jailed Chinese Nobel Peace Laureate Liu Xiaobo's tragic death at the hands of the Chinese government and his family's tremendous sufferings. The heartbreaking news of his passing just two days before our meeting today feels particularly cruel, but it is critical for us to take this time to discuss how we can still lend a helping hand to assist his family, and how we can fight to honor the legacy of Liu Xiaobo's courage and sacrifice.

Let me first say that Liu Xiaobo's tragedy represents the tragedies of many human rights activists in China, but it is also unique in its own way. In all of Nobel Peace Prize history, there have only been three jailed Laureates. But among them, Liu Xiaobo is perhaps the most tragic one.

During her house arrest, Aung San Suu Kyi was allowed some communication with the outside world, as she was occasionally allowed visits from foreign diplomats as well as from her personal physician. Even under the Nazis, Carl von Ossietzky was able to issue a note from the hospital where he was treated for tuberculosis to announce his decision to accept the Nobel Peace Prize in 1936.

But Liu Xiaobo was not able to do any of those in his nearly 9 years in prison. Liu Xiaobo had been held incommunicado since 2008, until he became terminally ill and was eventually allowed a visit by a German doctor and an American doctor after the pleas to Xi Jinping from both President Trump and German Chancellor Merkel. He was not allowed even to talk about any current affairs with his wife Liu Xia during her visits, nor the persecutions Liu Xia and her family suffered throughout Liu Xiaobo's imprisonment. Even on his deathbed, he had no freedom to leave his last words. Now that he is gone, the world will never know.

No doubt, our hero Liu Xiaobo faced one of the most evil and most inhumane regimes in the history of mankind. The international community could do nothing except watch this great freedom fighter slowly murdered by the regime in front of the world. That's the real tragedy.

Despite the Chinese regime's claim that Liu Xiaobo was diagnosed with advanced liver cancer in a regular physical checkup on May 31 and confirmed on June 7, an independent source told me that Liu Xiaobo's cancer was in fact diagnosed on May 23 during an emergency hospital visit because of internal bleeding, and since then he had been hospitalized in the First Hospital of China Medical University in Shenyang, Liaoning Province. However, the news of his late-stage cancer was not leaked out until the late June. During this time, his tumor enlarged from 5-6 cm to 11-12 cm.

When Liu Xiaobo's worsening condition became public, human rights activists, 154 Nobel laureates and world leaders called for Liu Xiaobo's immediate release and medical treatment overseas. Liu Xiaobo himself also expressed his wish to seek medical treatment abroad and to die in a free place. Unfortunately, the Chinese regime turned a deaf ear to these requests while the whole world watched. After suppressing and persecuting him for decades, China still didn't even hesitate to crush Liu Xiaobo's final wish.

Although the Chinese Communist regime approved his medical parole application, it still denied Liu Xiaobo's freedom of movement. He was closely guarded by the Chinese police 24/7 in the hospital. The regime not only banned Liu Xiaobo's friends from visiting him, but also threatened his family members and prohibited them from contacting the outside world.

Despite all the propaganda of so-called "meticulous care" the regime offered to Liu Xiaobo, his condition became life threatening, with multiple organ failures, including from respiratory and renal failure as well as septic shock, and in the end he succumbed to the cancer.

I strongly believe that the Chinese regime deliberately chose not to treat Liu Xiaobo's cancer earlier. As early as 2010, Liu Xiaobo was suspected of suffering from hepatitis B. His lawyers had been petitioning the government to grant medical parole so that Liu Xiaobo could treat his liver disease, but the Chinese authorities never allowed him proper diagnosis and treatment. The denial of medical care lead to Liu Xiaobo's advanced liver cancer, and was at its core a disguised death sentence.

Mr. Chairman, as you may know, in China it is not doctors but the party officials to decide whether to grant medical parole. In other words, medical parole in China is a political, not a medical decision. In Liu Xiaobo's case it was up to China's top leaders to decide. The party officials often deny many jailed activists' requests for medical parole, and the incarcerated activists often miss the opportunities to have early diagnosis and treatment. Some die while incarcerated. Human rights activist Cao Shunli was one, and now Liu Xiaobo has become another.

I believe there is clearly a pattern of the Chinese regime deliberately neglecting detained and jailed activists' health, mistreating them, including torture and forced ingestion of harmful drugs, as reported by jailed activists' family members or released activists.

It is reported that Liu Xiaobo had two CT tests last year. How can two tests fail to reveal Xiaobo's fairly large liver tumors? Many, including myself, suspect that the Chinese officials intentionally concealed this info from Liu Xiaobo and his family. This is why they have been withholding Liu Xiaobo's medical records from him and his family.

These records are classified as the top secret of the state. I think the international community should call for the release of Liu Xiaobo's medical records to his family and the experts that the family hired to examine this case.

To prevent Liu Xiaobo from seeking medical treatment overseas, China insisted that Liu Xiaobo was too ill to travel, and manipulated what medical experts from the U.S. and Germany said about Liu's treatment. But the two foreign doctors issued a joint statement, agreeing that Liu Xiaobo can be safely transported with appropriate medical evacuation care and support. They also warned that medical evacuation would have to take place as quickly as possible. This most recent event has demonstrated again the point that there is a pattern to allow activists to languish in the party's legal system.

I believe the reason that the Chinese regime denied Liu Xiaobo's wish and the world's appeal to allow him medical treatment abroad and to die in a free place is that it fears the truth of its ruthless persecution will come to light. The world media would focus on Liu Xiaobo and the regime's lies would be exposed. More and more people in China would see the true nature of this one-party state. The government would lose control.

No doubt, the Chinese Communist regime is responsible for Liu Xiaobo's worsening health and for his death. However, the Western countries' appeasement policy towards China's human rights abuses has made them accomplices of Liu Xiaobo's slow murder. If the world continues to acquiesce to China's aggression against its own people, appeasing the Chinese Communist Party without any moral clarity, Liu Xiaobo's tragedy will repeat, and more human rights activists will languish and disappear in Chinese prisons.

To change this, the international community must hold the Chinese regime and those individuals who mistreated Liu Xiaobo accountable.

Mr. Chairman, the U.S. can and should do more to help Liu Xiaobo and other human rights activists in China. For example, it can implement country-specific, and tougher sanctions against those personally responsible for Liu Xiaobo's death. The U.S. can use the Global Magnitsky Act as a tool to sanction them, banning them from traveling in the U.S. and freezing their assets in this country, and also encourage its allies to do the same. It should also consider trade sanctions. In addition, the U.S. can honor Liu Xiaobo's life and legacy by passing legislation to permanently rename the street in front of Chinese Embassy in Washington DC as "Liu Xiaobo Plaza."

To fight for the ideals of human rights and democracy, Liu Xiaobo gave up his career, he gave up his liberty, he gave up his freedom, and now, he has given up his life. But we cannot give up on Liu Xiaobo. We have to seek justice for Liu Xiaobo's death at the hands of the Chinese regime, and we have to preserve the legacy of Liu Xiaobo's struggle for a democratic China.

Mr. Chairman, now I'd like to turn your attention to the hypocrisy of the Chinese legal system. China's president Xi Jinping is boasting that China is a country that follows rule-of-law, where everyone stands equal before the law, but in reality, China's legal system is nothing but a fig leaf to cover the regime abuses and crimes against its own people.

The Chinese regime and its propaganda apparatus describe Liu Xiaobo as a "convicted criminal", but we all know Liu Xiaobo is innocent. He merely exercised his rights of free expression guaranteed under the Chinese Constitution, but he was deprived his freedom under the color of the law, and the regime falsified a crime and wrongfully sentenced him 11 years in prison.

As you may recall, Liu Xiaobo was a Chinese literary lecturer at my Alma mater Beijing Normal University. He was a leader in the heroic peaceful protests in the 1989 pro-democracy movement. He initiated a four-man three-day hunger strike on June 2nd, and at the massacre eve of June 3rd, Liu Xiaobo led a successful negotiation to get student protestors withdrawn from Tiananmen Square, and possibly saved several thousand students' lives. For that he was jailed for 19 months for counter-revolution activities.

Later Liu Xiaobo was arrested and convicted several times for his involvement in voicing publicly the need to redress the Tiananmen massacre, for his advocacy of peaceful unification with Taiwan, and for calling for political reform, greater human rights, and an end to one-party rule in China.

Liu Xiaobo led the effort in drafting Charter 08, a declaration to demand political reform. On December 8, 2008, police from Beijing police arrived at Liu Xiaobo's home around 11 p.m. and took Liu Xiaobo away and searched his home, confiscating computers and other materials. He was denied access to a lawyer until June 23, 2009, the date of his formal arrest, 7 months after his detention.

Liu Xiaobo was tried by the Beijing No. 1 Intermediate People's Court on December 23, 2009, and pleaded not guilty to the charge of "inciting subversion of state power" for co-authoring Charter 08. The trial lasted less than three hours, and the defense was not permitted to present evidence. Two days later, Liu Xiaobo was sentenced to 11 years in prison and two years' deprivation of political rights. The Beijing High Court rejected his appeal on February 11, 2010.

The court decision was only 11 pages, in which only five hundred words accounted for his charges and ruling over Liu Xiaobo's "instigation of others to subvert China's state power and the socialist system". The main evidence presented was Xiaobo's six articles published in Observer and BBC Chinese website between October 2005 to August 2007, and the court determined 223 characters in these six articles as criminal evidence against Liu Xiaobo.

In October 2010, Liu Xiaobo was awarded the Nobel Peace Prize for "his long and non-violent struggle for fundamental human rights in China." He was prohibited from attending his Nobel Award Ceremony by the Chinese government, and as a representative of Liu Xiaobo's family, I was part of the effort to recommend an empty chair in the ceremony to symbolize his presence.

Liu Xiaobo's Nobel Peace Prize brought not glory, but endless persecution for his wife Liu Xia, a well-known artist, and her family. While it is common practice to intimidate, monitor, threaten, torture, and sabotage the lives of not only dissidents themselves, but also their family members, the Chinese Communist regime has gone to extreme lengths to persecute Liu Xiaobo, Liu Xia, and her family.

Mr. Chairman, I would like to share with you the extent of the pain and persecutions that Liu Xia and her family have suffered as part of the political revenge that the Chinese government has taken against Liu Xiaobo.

Liu Xia has been isolated under house arrest ever since October 2010, the exact month that Liu Xiaobo was awarded the Nobel Peace Prize. Liu Xia's freedom of movement has been severely restricted. Her friends and visitors are not allowed to see her. She has no phone or internet access and extremely limited outside contact with the world.

On several occasions, Liu Xia was close to a nervous breakdown and she suffers from very severe depression. Liu Xia also suffers from a serious heart condition, for which she was sent to a hospital in 2014 and told that her heart was lacking blood. Her condition has continuously worsened over the years due to the distressing environment of persecution, extended isolation from loved ones, and because authorities prevent her from seeking medical treatment overseas. Liu Xiaobo chose to defend freedom of speech and democracy, Liu Xia fell in love with Liu Xiaobo, and just for this, the Chinese government put her into an invisible prison where she continues to suffer unbelievable psychological torment.

Technically Liu Xia is a free person, not in violation of any Chinese law, nor charged with any crimes by the government. Her only "crime" is she is the wife of a Nobel Peace Prize winner, for which she has been punished and made a prisoner in her own house for nearly seven years.

Liu Xia is followed 24/7 by the police and her apartment is also closely guarded by a hired security team. Even as she cared for her husband in the hospital in the past weeks, she was still followed by a police security team. She is not allowed to work and has no choice but to rely on their savings and other family members' financial support to get by.

Her older brother Liu Tong, used to be the CEO of a prosperous IT company. The government forced him to sell his company, which caused the loss of millions of dollars in assets. Police constantly harass him and his family. His wife has no choice but to abandon a good job and find sanctuary in the United States. Liu Tong is forbidden from traveling outside of China, and cannot join his wife and son here in this country, even though he has never convicted any crime, and is supposedly guaranteed a right for freedom of movement by the Chinese Constitution. To further punish the family, Liu Tong was banned to visit Liu Xiaobo in the hospital even in his last days of life.

Liu Xia's younger brother Liu Hui had financially supported Liu Xia and been a messenger between her and Liu Xiaobo's lawyers. In 2013, the government falsified an economic crime against Liu Hui and sentenced him to 11 years in prison. He suffers from diabetes and high blood pressure, but was denied medical care during his sentence. He even suffered a stroke and almost died in prison. Now, he is still on parole. Rights lawyers, activists, and family members all saw Liu Hui's conviction as politically motivated revenge on Liu Xiaobo and Liu Xia. At the time of the trial, Nicholas Bequelin, currently the East Asia Regional Director of Amnesty International, said: "This is not a normal case making its way through the judicial system. This case is retaliation and is designed to coerce [Liu Xia] into silence... It's so nakedly unlawful and egregious."

During the span of her house arrest, Liu Xia's aging parents had been constantly harassed and worried. Both passed away successively in fear and in agony.

The tragic case of Liu Xiaobo is not a single tragedy. It has caused a chain reaction of tragedies that shattered Liu Xia's extended family, and made all the family members into victims of the regime, for the "crime" of relation and the "crime" of love. But in this process of abuse, the Chinese government has created a tragedy for itself too. It has displayed the ugly face of its obsession with control and its utter disregard for human rights for the entire world to see.

Thank you.

II

Washington Post Article   Dear
President Trump: Please Let Liu Xiaobo Die As a Free Man
The Nobel Peace Prize Laureate Has Devoted His Life to the Cause of Freedom in China.

June 27, 2017

By Jared Genser and Yang Jianli

On Monday, China released Nobel Peace Prize laureate Liu Xiaobo from prison on parole, after he was diagnosed as being in the final stages of liver cancer. He is being treated at a hospital in the northeastern city of Shenyang, but he has asked Chinese authorities to let him travel to the United States with his wife, Liu Xia, for medical treatment. President Trump should immediately urge Chinese President Xi Jinping to grant Liu's request on humanitarian grounds.
It is incredibly disturbing that the Chinese government failed to diagnose its most famous political prisoner as having cancer until it was too late for meaningful treatment. Liu Xiaobo is a scholar and democracy activist who was imprisoned primarily for his role in drafting Charter 08, a political manifesto that called for greater rule of law, respect for

human rights and an end to one-party rule in China. He was detained two days before the public release of Charter 08, and in December 2009, he was sentenced to 11 years in prison for "inciting subversion of state power."

On Oct. 8, 2010, the Norwegian Nobel Committee announced that Liu was the recipient of the Nobel Peace Prize. Within two weeks, Liu Xia was placed under house arrest and has been held without charge or trial for almost seven years.

Liu Xiaobo's imprisonment coincided with China's rise as a global power on the world stage. In recent years, China has raised its military budget past a record high of $145 billion annually and vigorously contested competing claims in the South China Sea. In its "One Belt, One Road Initiative," China is investing hundreds of billions of dollars into infrastructure projects across Asia, Africa and Europe. And it has created the Asian Infrastructure Investment Bank, whose 57 members have contributed more than $100 billion, making it half the size of its rival World Bank. It has also positioned itself to be a key interlocutor with difficult states such as Iran and North Korea.

At home, however, Xi has faced serious economic and environmental challenges, as best highlighted by an extraordinary rise in domestic dissent. In response, Xi has unabashedly increased repression of religious and ethnic minorities, human rights lawyers and civil society activists; China reportedly now spends more than $120 billion annually on domestic security.

As China's power and influence have increased, Western democracies have collectively engaged in self-censorship on human rights, choosing to prioritize what they have clearly believed to be their more important interests over their purported values. In the past five years, since Xi became president, discussions on human rights have been relegated to fruitless dialogues with the Chinese foreign ministry, which has never had any power over domestic concerns.

President Barack Obama led the West in playing down concerns with China on human rights and was conspicuous by his unwillingness to help Liu, his fellow Nobel Peace Prize laureate. He raised Liu Xiaobo's case publicly only once after he was awarded the Nobel Peace Prize, and whatever he might have said privately clearly had no impact. At the same time, he did not join 134 Nobel laureates on a letter to Xi, did not publicly condemn Liu Xia's detention under house arrest and even threatened to veto a bill, passed by the Senate, to rename the street in front of the Chinese Embassy "Liu Xiaobo Plaza."

Chinese security officials even exploited the United States' repeated refusal to help the Lius in torture sessions with detained Chinese dissidents. They explained to their victims that they surely must have observed that Washington had refused to help the world's only imprisoned Nobel Peace Prize laureate and his wife – so what hope could they expect if they were to be disappeared, tortured or imprisoned? The American refusal of support to the Lius gave Xi license to act with total impunity to repress domestic dissent.

Much as that unknown protester stood in front of the tank in Tiananmen Square, Liu Xiaobo volunteered to be the first signatory of Charter 08, knowing that by symbolizing the Chinese people's demands for human rights, democracy and the rule of law, he would pose a singular threat to the one-party system. For that courageous stand, he paid with his and his wife's freedom, and he is about to pay with his life.

Now is the time for Trump and the United States to honor his sacrifice and his dying wishes and to implore Chinese authorities to allow him to obtain medical treatment here and live out his remaining days in freedom.

Jared Genser, founder of Freedom Now, is pro bono counsel to Liu Xiaobo and Liu Xia. Yang Jianli is president of Initiatives for China.

III

Democracy for China: Missed Opportunities and Opportunities Ahead
Speech at the Congressional Defense and Foreign Policy Forum Hosted by Defense Forum Foundation.

by: YANG Jianli

June 17, 2016

Thank you so much, Suzanne, for such a kind and generous introduction. The only problem was that, hearing the introduction, I thought I was dead. But I cannot and shouldn't think that, for my mission is not yet finished.

I am honored to be invited by the Defense Forum Foundation, and specifically by its Chairman, Ambassador Middendorf.

I was impressed to learn that Ambassador Middendorf did such a good job as President Ford's Secretary of the Navy that President Carter paid him the unusual tribute of asking him to remain as Secretary.

I also admire the many years of efforts by DFF's President Suzanne Scholte to expose human rights abuses, especially in North Korea, which surpasses even China in the primitive brutality of its repression. Suzanne invited me to speak more than 7 years ago about Charter 08 not long after it was published. Charter 08 is a manifesto led by Liu Xiaobo demanding a peaceful democratic transition in China, for which Liu Xiaobo was arrested and sentenced to 11 years in prison, and for his leadership role in Charter 08 and two decades of peaceful struggle to advance human rights and democracy, he won the 2010 Nobel Peace Prize. But I want to remind everyone that as I speak he is still languishing in China's prison.

Thank you, Suzanne, for inviting me back to talk about China's democratic perspectives. Can you think of any topic harder than this?

I personally think the three most difficult things facing humanity are: making peace in the Middle East, democratizing China, and losing weight. Unfortunately, I am taking up two of the three.

Let's go back to the most important reference point in talking about Chinese politics–the 1989 Tiananmen incident, whose 27th anniversary we just commemorated less than two weeks ago.

The 1989 pro-democracy movement stood against government corruption and for democracy and freedom. This movement was widespread but ended in bloodshed. The Tiananmen massacre created a strong sense of fear and dismay of general politics among ordinary people. Any room for a public system of checks and balances against governmental abuse of power was taken away.

It also created a sense of fear and crisis within the Communist regime, because it had brought unprecedented public awareness to human rights and democracy. Life was no longer the same for the rulers who had to face a completely different domestic and international environment.

The subsequent disintegration of the Soviet Union and the Eastern European Bloc cast an even heavier cloud over the heads of Chinese Communist officials. "How long can the red flag continue to fly?" They all started to doubt.

To be sure, the CCP regime was struggling to survive the Tiananmen crisis, for which breaking international isolation was one of the imperatives facing the regime. Less than three weeks after the Massacre when China's leadership was least assertive and most susceptible to outside pressures, President Bush secretly sent his special envoy National Security Adviser Brent Scowcroft to meet with Deng Xiaoping and other Chinese leaders.

The meeting, later made public, did not seem to bring about any tangible results for either side. But this very gesture of President Bush's reveled America's weakness and assured China's leadership the US's intention to continue the recognition of, and maintain the normal relations with, the repressive regime even if there was no indication of its willingness to admit or correct its serious mistakes or crimes. On July 28, 3 weeks after his special envoy returned to Washington, President Bush wrote a second, extremely carefully worded letter to Deng Xiaoping. "Please understand", wrote Bush, "that this letter has been personally written, and is coming from one who wants to go forward together. Please don't be angry with me if I have crossed the invisible threshold laying between constructive suggestion and 'internal interference'..." What could that imply? Judge for yourselves.

Democrats, especially Governor Bill Clinton in his campaign trail, harshly criticized Bush for "kowtowing" to China, while some conservatives saw Bush's move in the aftermath of the Tiananmen incident as premature in the absence of conciliatory gestures from Beijing. Different China views were reflected in the debate on whether and how to continue to grant China a MFN trade status.

One side of the debate, led by Rep. Nancy Pelosi and Senator George Mitchell, asserted that US trade relations with China must be linked to China's human rights record. We, Chinese democracy activists, supported this idea because we understood that without such a linkage, continuing normal trade with China would be like a blood transfusion to the CCP regime, making it more aggressive and harming the interests of both the American and Chinese people. This idea was embodied in Pelosi and Mitchell's legislation in 1993. But one year after assuming presidency, President Clinton took a 180 degree turn and reversed the policy. The reversal was based on the theory, which was widely upheld by corporations, columnists, pundits and policy makers, that trade would lead to democracy because trade would inevitably result in economic growth and the growth of the middle class which would in turn demand more political freedom.

This theory does not seem to apply to China, at least up to this point.

With money and technology pouring in from the U.S. and other Western countries, the Chinese Communist regime not only survived the 1989 crisis, it catapulted into the 21st century. The country's explosive economic growth lifted it from one of the poorest countries to become the number two economy in the world; but China remains firmly near the bottom of indicators on democratic development. Over the years China's middle class have largely been acquiescent to its one-party dictatorship and its gross violations of human rights. What has gone wrong, in China and the international community?

Let's look at China.

In 1992, when the Americans were heatedly debating about China policy and about to delink human rights from trade, Deng Xiaoping took the famous Southern Inspection Tour to further economic opening up. Communist officials at all levels soon realized three realities: First, the Chinese Communist Party's stay in power has nothing to do with communist ideals. Second, "economic growth means everything;" that is, continued economic growth is the last, best hope to keep the CCP ship afloat. Third, in order to uphold the one-party dictatorship, it had to rely on capitalizing on the dark and evil side of human nature: spoiling the elite in exchange for their loyalty.

With the understanding of these three realities, the communist officials developed an undocumented but almost unanimously accepted code of conduct-or rather, code of corruption. So, every piece of governmental power is on sale in the market and every corner of the market is invaded by political power.

Officials in all government agencies spent most of their energy beefing up GDP, engaging in power arbitrage, bribing their superiors, and seeking luxurious personal perks. As a result, the Communist Party elite, who used to label themselves "the vanguards of the proletariat class," had either turned themselves into get-rich-overnight capitalists, or become brokers, patrons, and backers of domestic and foreign capitalists.

In such a political environment, political power was dancing a full-swing tango with capital operation. Low human rights standards, low wages, lack of environmental protection regulations and enforcement, and the illegality of collective bargaining all contributed to creating a golden opportunity for domestic and international speculative capitalists. As a result, "money" quickly courted "political power." Business venture takers would go to any length to seek out someone in power to serve as backers so that they could grab market opportunities without fair competition. They also used political connections to shed any and all legal and social responsibility. In a sense, the Chinese

Communist Party, which used to be China Inc.'s sole shareholder, had now opened up its equity and offered its shares for capitalists to purchase.

This is very important for one to understand why "the middle class prediction" has so far failed in China.

One. Given China's government-market relations, the middle class owed its success to the privileged relations with the state. To expect such a state-dependent class to make bold political claims would have been fanciful.

Two. Trade and economic development were carried out as a matter of deliberate state policy, unlike the US and UK these early developed countries which developed without knowing, the fast growth did not give rise to a politically independent middle class, but instead allowed the existing ruling structure to absorb into its own ranks the most talented and ambitious members of business elite. The CCP's 16th National Congress, for example, published a new Party Charter that welcomed capitalists as Party members.

Meanwhile, the shares of China, Inc. were offered to China's intellectuals as free, performance-related stock options. In order to sustain stability, the CCP regime offered all kinds of bribery incentives to buy off anyone and everyone of importance and influence in society. The bribery list includes bureaucrats at every level, military officers, and business leaders as well as college professors, journalists, publishers, authors, art performers, high-profile athletes, and so on. The government pays all these people off in the form of salaries, bonuses, state-covered expenses, free medical insurance, subsidized housing, free pension plans and so on. Laws and policies more and more favor this group of people in exchange for their recognition and acceptance of the political status quo. Their income and perks add up to wealth that is disproportionally higher than that of ordinary workers, farm workers, clerks, and small business owners. Such a policy of co-opting and buying off potential opposition was quite effective in conjunction with the purges and persecution after the Tiananmen massacre. The cruelty of political reality created terror in the minds of intellectuals as a psychological deterrent. As time went on, fear turned into the cynicism, they became increasingly indifferent to what was right and what was wrong. Indifference and hypocrisy rapidly became a new fashion that the modern Chinese intellect tried to follow. This, coupled with a piece of the action in China Inc., made many intellectuals-who had once been independent and once been considered the conscience of the society-soften up their position against the post-1989 status quo.

Over the 1990's and the first 10 years of the 21st century, in China, power (political elite), capital (economic elite) and "intellect" (social and cultural elite), were bonded together and formed an alliance that is maintaining the existing political order. This alliance owns and runs China, Inc., dazzling the entire world with its wealth, might and glory. With China's vast geographic size and population, the shareholders of China, Inc. have impressed many observers with their prodigious wealth accumulation and astonishing growth rates, making those same observers believe that one-party dictatorship is good for economic growth. By the same token, these shareholders also control all the channels of the information flow and dominate the public discourse. They can make their voices loud enough so the outside observers believe that they represent China, that they are China-the whole of China.

The truth is, there is another society named China, a society constituted of over a billion Chinese who are virtually laborers working for China, Inc. and whose basic rights are almost totally disregarded, the China that people sarcastically call "the China of shitizens."

This was the China's two-China structure I often talked about before Xi Jinping took the power. This was largely a two-player game.

During the same period, the US diplomatic establishment largely harbored the delusion that economic growth will bring about democracy in China. US Presidents and other senior officials, deeming human rights issues inconvenient while engaging with China, would avoid them as much as they could. Faced with the rising China, US gradually lost leverages. Now, the Chinese leadership practically cares little about the pressure from Western public opinion because politicians and businessmen from around the world are salivating at China's immense purchasing power, investment and markets. It's no exaggeration to say that today, Chinese leaders are the most well-received, honored guests in a majority of countries worldwide; China is the destination for many of the world's elite who thirst for gold.

Beijing tightly controls the freedom of the press. They could cut off Google and Yahoo anytime; they'd refused visas for New York Times journalists and critical scholars, and blocked access to Twitter and Facebook. All with impunity. While at the same time, they can set up any media they would like in the US. Ironically, China, which screens, censors and bans any print and electronic publication, has been invited to serve as the country of honor at book fairs in Frankfurt, London, and New York! Hollywood is the epitome of free American culture; filmmakers are free to ridicule, mock, and criticize American politicians and government officials such as senators, judges, and the president, without fear of persecution. But in their pursuit of China's box office dollars, Hollywood executives have consciously decided to steer clear of any criticism of the Chinese government. Despite this, American movies are still censored in China, and some are not allowed at all. Virtually all American media are blocked in China. In the United States today, the Chinese government and its surrogates have wide access to universities, think tanks, and broadcast studios through which they can advance their opinions and rationalize their actions.

China is using the economic power it has gained with the help of the West to build a formidable, modern military. As its power grows, China is demanding a re-write of international norms and rules. China wants to create a new international order with China at the center of the Asia-Pacific region, bringing regional and world peace under threat. The current South China Sea tension is just a case in point.

In short, the failure of the US to proactively seek advancement of human rights and democracy in China has in turn harmed its long term national interest and its democratic way of life.

Let's look at China again to examine opportunities ahead of us.

Despite his unprecedented high-profiled anti-corruption effort, Xi Jinping has largely continued the two China structure and shown the world that he is more determined than his predecessors not to abandon the one-party dictatorship in favor of democratic reforms.

A important change albeit subtle change, however, is taking place largely due to Xi Jinping's personality, anti-corruption campaign and the unstoppable economic down turn.

Xi Jinping has concentrated power in his own hands and built a cult of personality. The Economist writes that Xi is now not the CEO (the chief executive officer) but the COE, the "Chairman of Everything." He's the head of state, the leader of the Communist Party, the commander-in-chief of the armed forces, the head of the security services, the head of the committee in charge of the so-called "comprehensive reform," and also the person in charge of the economy.

He has abolished the practice of "collective leadership," which was adopted in 1982 to prevent a return to the totalitarian terror of Mao's unchecked dictatorship, which produced such horrors as the Cultural Revolution. All this has undergone through power struggles in form of anticorruption campaign. In doing so he has alienated his comrades at all levels and they have remained in a "state of idle" to quietly protest. One of the major reasons behind Xi's anticorruption campaign is the two-China ruling model--co-opting the elite and exchanging corruption for loyalty, has become increasingly costly and thus almost unbearable. But ending that model without granting people more liberties is an impossible task. The only thing it can achieve is to alienate the political, business, intellectual elite, the middle class if you will. With the economic down turn, more and more members of the middle class are feeling insecure and seeking to leave the ruling structure and even the country.

At the same time, Xi, acting out of fear, has overseen the harshest crackdown on dissent since the Tiananmen massacre, arresting lawyers, academics, workers, and civil society activists, and tightening controls over the media and access to the Internet.

Politically, the elite who are just beginning to turn their backs on the regime, are caught between a ruling party above, and a mass of workers and peasants below, with whom there is no mutual trust.

Xi Jinping is a game changer. He is unwittingly turning the two player game into a three player game, dissolving the power base that has helped the party stay in power to this day. This is the deepest crisis facing the Xi Jinping regime.

To be sure, growth is slowing; the party is in disarray, because the rules it has established to limit internecine political warfare have collapsed; Beijing's foreign policy is driving the Sino-U.S. relationship toward conflict; middle-class acquiescence is beginning to erode.

But I do not pretend that revolution will take place tomorrow. We must be noted it usually takes four factors to be present at the same time to begin a real democratic transition in an autocratic country: 1) general robust disaffection from people; 2) split in the leadership in the autocratic regime; 3) viable democratic opposition; and 4) international support.

Let me elaborate.

First. China's Stability Sustaining System treats every citizen as a potential enemy, and it has successfully made them enemies–dissidents, independent intellectuals, land-lease peasants, victims of forced demolitions and eviction, victims of forced abortion, veterans, migrant workers, Tibetans, Uyghurs, Mongolians, Christians, and Falun Gong practitioners, you name it. The CCP regime does not lack enemies. With slower economic growth, the grievances of the shitizens will be laid barer and social unrests can only be mounting.

Second. As I said earlier, the elite China is beginning to decompose. Party's leadership unity has also disintegrated, as shown by the purge of Bo Xilai, Ling Jihua, Zhou Yongkang and their cronies since 2012.

Perhaps the only achievement in China's political system in the past 30 years is the establishment of the "two-term, 10-year, one-generation" term limit system. Many observers predicted that such a system would ensure long-term stability for the CCP regime, wishfully believing that this system helped the CCP find a way out of the pit of power discontinuity that has plagued all dictatorships in history. The Bo Xilai incident, however, mercilessly burst that bubble. Now it is Xi Jinping himself that is challenging this norm. The cracks within the party are only widening.

Third. The concept of democracy has prevailed in the minds of the general public, thanks to the dozens years of efforts made by the pro-democratic activists both in and outside of China.

In the meantime, the ordinary people are becoming more mature, more skillful, and more aggressive in fighting for their own civil rights. Generally speaking, as citizen forces grow and the civil protests escalate, struggle for power among different factions with the communist regime will become public. Especially, once the external pressure reaches a critical mass, the rivalry factions with the CCP will have to take the citizen force into serious account and seek or use the latter's support.

That said, I want to emphasize that we need an overall, viable pro-democracy movement to force the dictatorship to crack open. A milestone to meet that objective would be the formation of a group of civil leaders able to represent the general public, integrating the middle class and lower class people in demanding for democracy, and to at least partially disrupt the current political order — a group that will catch attention and support of the international community and can carry out and to call for effective negotiations with the government.

Fourth, last but not least, international support.

China under one-party dictatorship cannot rise peacefully, and its transition to a democratic country that respects human rights, rule of law, freedom of speech and religion, is in everyone's best interest, including America. In other words, the U.S. must push for a peaceful democratic transition in China. The reason for this is simple: To support China's regime, a regime that ruthlessly represses its own people, denies universal values to justify its dictatorship, and challenges the existing international order to seek its dominance, is morally corrupt as well as strategically unsound. Like Frankenstein's monster, China is now seeking to revenge against its creator – the West.

While many policymakers in Washington have now realized that it is time to get tough on China, some still believe that the present and future conflicts between the U. S. and China can be managed. My view is this: Without China's democratization, a clash between the U. S. and China is unavoidable because the two countries' strategic goals are on a clashing course and their core interests cannot be compromised.

I hereby call the US to end the compartmentalization of human rights and begin to engage China with moral and strategic clarity.

To start, the Congress should pass a China Democracy Act that flatly states that enhancing human rights and democratic transition in China is decidedly in America's national interest and that directs the Federal government and all its agencies to make democracy and human rights advocacy the core of all engagement with China. This would be binding legislation precluding the currently widespread but inaccurate claim that Congress must balance, on the one hand, it's claim to support the universal value of human rights, and, on the other hand, "America's national interest." The bill also would require a report from the President to Congress every year on how any government program, policy, or action during the prior twelve months has strengthened or weakened human rights and democratic values in China.

All federal departments of government – every single one – should have to report on what they're doing to bring democracy to China by advancing human rights and the rule of law there. The Act also put them on notice to take no action, adopt no policy and implement no program that would undercut the democracy movement, or weaken human rights in China.

Such a China Democracy Act will give us a better idea of what successes we've had so far, what caused them, and how we should increase financial resources and deploy them to promote democracy and human rights.

Such an Act will serve as America's grand strategy toward China, setting a firm foundation that not only guides U. S. activities with China in all spheres, but also makes clear of the U. S. intentions to the Chinese government and sends an unequivocal message of support to the Chinese people.

No one can predict with precision when the moment of dramatic opening for change will come in China. Virtually every one of the sixty some peaceful transitions to democracy in the past few decades have come as a surprise to the US.

Above all else we must maintain our faith in my compatriots that they can and will join the vast majority of the world's peoples who now live in free or at least partly free countries. An opening for change could come in the next few months or it may take a few more years. But it will never come without collective efforts, including those from the international community. So we must persevere and keep the faith and be ready.

Perhaps, Suzanne, you will invite me to speak at this forum again in 7 years. If so, it is my hope that by that time the China Democracy Act will have long been enacted and my topic will be Perspectives of Consolidating China's Nascent Democracy.

Thank you all.

Mr. SMITH. Dr. Yang, thank you for your eloquent and moving and enlightened recommendations and testimony.

Mr. Genser.

STATEMENT OF MR. JARED GENSER, FOUNDER, FREEDOM NOW

Mr. GENSER. Thanks so much, Mr. Chairman, Ranking Member Bass. It is with a heavy heart and after a tragic day yesterday that I appear before you this morning.

Undoubtedly, Yang Jianli and Perry Link, who were friends with Liu Xiaobo, will be able to bring to life who he was as a person and will be able to speak better than me to his life and to his legacy. Sadly, I never met Liu Xiaobo, and now I never will

The intersection of my life with Liu Xiaobo came only after he had been convicted and sentenced to 11 years in prison for inciting subversion of state power. I was introduced to Liu Xia by my friend and colleague Yang Jianli.

It was Jianli, among many others, who 20 years ago inspired me to become a human rights lawyer, as we helped organize the protest against Jiang Zemin when he visited Harvard in the fall of 1997. And 5 years later I served as Jianli's lawyer when he was detained in China and faced a death sentence on the pretextual charge of being a spy for Taiwan. It was in mid-2010 that I was introduced by Jianli to Liu Xia.

What I can uniquely speak about today, however, is the brutality of the Chinese Government and its fear of change, for I have seen through the intense and unrelenting persecution of Liu Xiaobo and Liu Xia some of the most horrific, callous, and inhuman acts that go beyond the power of an ordinary and normal person's power of imagination.

Over the summer of 2010 I got to know Liu Xia as we began preparing to take her husband's case to the United Nations. As the announcement of the Nobel Peace Prize approached that year it was rumored he was on the short list, and Liu Xia and I discussed if it made more sense for her to travel abroad to fight for her husband's freedom or to remain in China. Despite the concerns I expressed to her that she would not likely remain free if Liu won the prize, she told me unequivocally, "My place is in China with my husband."

Shortly after he was announced as the recipient of the prize in October 2010, the security cordon came down and she was placed under house arrest, and she has been held without charge or trial ever since.

I had the tremendous privilege and honor to represent the Lius in Oslo and to sit in the front row as the prize was presented to the empty chair. But I know and I knew on that day that the prize was awarded that getting them both out would be a virtually impossible task.

For myself, while I expected her ability to communicate or travel to be restricted, I never could have imagined how much the Chinese Government would punish Liu Xia for the crime of being married to her husband.

She was held in a one-bedroom apartment in Beijing, one of the most popular cities in the world, and for the first several years virtually incommunicado, with a security guard posted outside of her door and security at the front of the building to turn people away. She had no telephone, no Internet access, and was only able to see her parents once a month and was taken to see Liu Xiaobo once a month. She suffered severe depression and had a heart attack. On a handful of occasions journalists broke through the security cordon, captured brief images of her, clearly in intense agony. To punish her for these incidents the Chinese Government prosecuted her brother Liu Hui on bogus economic crimes charges and sen- tenced him to 11 years in prison, and he served some 2 years-plus in jail. She was captured by one journalist and she was taken to his trial crying out, "Tell the world I am not free."

In her latter years under house arrest and with her own health deteriorating rapidly, she was allowed to be in touch with a very small number of friends, but the pressure on her was unrelenting. We don't know anything, anything at all, about how Liu Xiaobo has been treated in prison. The last time he said anything that was reported publicly was when he was sentenced to prison in Decem- ber 2009. All we know is that he was held in extended solitary con- finement throughout this time, which constitutes torture under international law, and we know that Liu Xia was able to visit him monthly, and we know that with all of its resources at the disposal of the Chinese Government it neglected his medical care so much so that it had no idea he had liver cancer until it had reached Stage 4 and was terminal.

As the Lius' counsel I fought their cases aggressively in every forum that I could find. We took their cases to the U.N. Working Group on Arbitrary Detention, and in response to our submission, the Chinese Government remarked regarding Liu Xia's detention, regarding her Kafkaesque existence, that she was "under no legal restriction."

That was perhaps actually literally true. She had been held actu- ally illegally without charge or trial now for almost 7 years. The U.N. found that they were both held arbitrarily and in violation of international law.

We secured a letter from 134 Nobel laureates urging President Xi to let them go, which was joined by 450,000 people around the world whose petitions we had delivered to a half dozen Chinese Embassies. And we published countless op-eds, testified before par- liaments, held candlelight vigils, and did everything possible to persuade governments around the world to act.

In the last few weeks we have seen President Xi and the Chinese Government at its worst.

First, their leaders were pressured not to tell anybody about Liu Xiaobo's cancer diagnosis.

Second, when they were able to make it public they were held virtually incommunicado at the hospital.

Third, the Chinese Government flagrantly lied about his condi- tions to the international community to justify him not being able to travel abroad for medical treatment.

Fourth, after a German and American doctor found he would have actually been able to travel abroad and there were treatments that could have extended his life for several weeks, the Chinese hospital published a statement asserting that the doctors, those foreign doctors, had actually said that he had gotten excellent care and was too sick to travel abroad.

Once the foreign doctors put out their own statement refuting what the Chinese hospital said, the government retreated back to telling the international community not to interfere with its internal affairs.

And fifth, as if Liu Xiaobo and Liu Xia had not suffered enough, in his dying days not only were family and friends denied the ability to visit and to tell him good-bye, but they were never even allowed to be alone with each other. The entire time, a Chinese security official was with them around the clock. And in the end, President Xi showed no humanity and no mercy.

If this is how China treats its most famous political prisoner, it is self-evident that the brutality of the Chinese Government in repressing its own population is as complete as it is unapologetic. Truly anything can be justified in the name of the greater good.

Yet despite the tragedy that Liu's freedom has come from his death, it is clear today that the Chinese Government has lost. Liu's ideas and his dreams will persist, spread, and will one day come to fruition. And his courage and his sacrifice for his country will inspire millions of Chinese activists and dissidents to persevere until China has become the multiparty democracy that Liu knew to his core was within its people's grasps.

So what do we do from here? The work is clearly not done in so many different respects. First and most immediately, the world must rescue Liu Xia. She must immediately be allowed to have open communication with the outside world, and her wishes for the burial of her husband and relocation of herself and her family must be fully honored. Given Xia is under "no legal restriction," this should be easy to achieve.

Second, the world must never forget Liu Xiaobo and what he stood for. I would urge all freedom-loving countries around the world, starting with the United States, to rename the street in front of the Chinese Embassy Liu Xiaobo Plaza. The Chinese Government is literally erasing him from existence in China. If you type his name in Chinese in the WeChat program online, for example, his name is instantly erased. The Chinese Government should never be allowed to forget Liu Xiaobo.

And finally, the best way to honor the legacy of Liu Xiaobo would be for the United States and so many other countries around the world to stand in solidarity with the Chinese people's struggle for freedom, democracy, and human rights.

As I noted before, the last time the world heard from Liu was in a statement released his by his counsel on December 25, 2009, right after he was sentenced to 11 years' imprisonment. Liu said, "I have long been aware that when an independent intellectual stands up to an autocratic state step one toward freedom is often a step into prison. Now I am taking that step, and true freedom is that much nearer."

It is tragic that Liu was only free when his soul left his body, but the legacy he left behind will never be forgotten.

Thank you.

[The prepared statement of Mr. Genser follows:]

House Foreign Affairs
Subcommittee on Africa, Global Health, Global Human Rights, and International Organizations

The Tragic Case of Liu Xiaobo

Friday, July 14, 2017

2172 Rayburn House Office Building

Testimony of Jared Genser[1]

Mr. Chairman and Members of the Subcommittee. It is with a heavy heart and after a tragic day yesterday that I appear before you this morning.

Undoubtedly, Yang Jianli and Perry Link, who were friends with Liu Xiaobo, will be able to bring to life who he was as a person and will be able to speak to his life and legacy. Sadly, I never met Liu Xiaobo and I now never will. The intersection of my life with Liu Xiaobo came only after he had been convicted and sentenced to 11 years in prison for "inciting subversion of state power." I was introduced to Liu Xia by my friend and colleague Yang Jianli. It was Jianli who among others inspired me to become a human-rights lawyer when as graduate students some 20 years ago, we organized the protests against Chinese President Jiang Zemin at Harvard University. Five years later, I served as Jianli's lawyer when he was detained in China and faced a death sentence for the pre-textual charge of being a spy for Taiwan. And in mid-2010, Jianli introduced me to Liu Xia.

What I can uniquely speak to today, however, is the brutality of the Chinese government and its fear of change. For I have seen through its intense and unrelenting persecution of Liu Xiaobo and Liu Xia some of the most horrific, callous, and inhuman acts that go beyond the power of an ordinary and normal person's power of imagination.

Over the summer of 2010, I got to know Liu Xia as we began preparing to take Liu Xiaobo's case to the United Nations. As the announcement of the Nobel Peace Prize approached that year, it was rumored he was on the short list. Liu Xia and I discussed if it made more sense for her to travel abroad to fight for his freedom or remain in China. Despite the concerns I expressed to her that she would not likely remain free if Liu won the prize, she told me unquivocally, "My place is in China with my husband." Shortly after he was announced as the recipient of the prize in October 2010, the security cordon came down and she was placed under house arrest. She has been held without charge or

---

[1] Founder, Freedom Now, and International Counsel to Liu Xioabo. For further information contact jgenser@freedom-now.org or 202-320-4135.

trial ever since. I had the tremendous privilege and honor to represent the Lius in Oslo and sit in the front row as the prize was presented to the empty chair. But I knew on the day the Prize was awarded that getting them both out would be a virtually impossible challenge.

For myself, while I expected her ability to communicate or travel to be restricted, I never could have imagine how much the Chinese government would punish Liu Xia for the crime of being married to her husband. She was held in a one-bedroom apartment in Beijing, one of the most populous cities in the world, for the first several years virtually *incommunicado*, with a security guard posted outside her door and security at the front of the building to turn people away. She had no telephone, no Internet access, and was only able to see her parents once a month and was taken to visit Liu Xiaobo once a month. She suffered severe depression and had a heart attack. On a handful of occasions journalists broke through the security cordon and captured brief images of her, clearly in intense agony. To punish her for these incidents, the Chinese government prosecuted her brother Liu Hui on bogus economic crimes charges and sentenced him to 11 years in prison. He served some two years in jail. She was captured by one journalist as she was taken to his trial crying out "Tell the world I'm not free." In her latter years under house arrest and with her own health deteriorating rapidly, she was able to be in touch with a very small number of friends. But the pressure on her was unrelenting.

We don't know anything – anything at all – about how Liu Xiaobo has been treated in prison. The last time he said anything that was reported publicly was when he was sentenced to prison in December 2009. All we know is that he was held in extended solitary confinement throughout this time, which constitutes torture under international law, we know that Liu Xia was able to visit him monthly, and we know that the Chinese government, with all of its resources so neglected his medical care that it had no idea he had liver cancer until it had reached Stage 4 and was terminal.

As the Lius' counsel, I fought their cases aggressively in every forum that I could find. We took their cases to the UN Working Group on Arbitrary Detention. In response to our submission, the Chinese government remarked regarding Liu Xia about her Kafka-esque existence she was "under no legal restriction." That was, perhaps, literally true. She has been held illegally, without charge or trial, for almost seven years. The UN found that they were both being held arbitrarily and in violation of international law. We secured a letter from 134 Nobel Laureates urging President Xi to let them go and that was joined by 450,000 people whose petitions were delivered to a half-dozen Chinese embassies. And we published countless opeds, testified before parliaments, held candlelight vigils, and did everything possible to persuade governments around the world to act.

In the last few weeks, we have seen President Xi and the Chinese government at its worst. First, the Lius were pressured not to tell anyone about Liu Xiaobo's cancer diagnosis. Second, when they were able to make it public, they were held virtually *incommunicado* at the hospital. Third, the Chinese government flagrantly lied about his conditions to the international community to justify him not being able to travel abroad for medical treatment. Fourth, after an American and German doctor found he would have been able to travel abroad and that there were treatments that could have extended his life for several weeks, the Chinese hospital published a statement asserting the doctor's said he had gotten excellent care and was too sick to travel abroad. Once the foreign doctors put out their own statement, the Chinese government just retreated back into telling the international community not to interfere in its internal affairs. And fifth, as if Liu Xiaobo and Liu Xia had not suffered enough, in his dying days not only were family and friends denied the ability to visit and tell him goodbye, but they were never allowed to be alone with each other -- the entire time a Chinese security official was with them around the clock. In the end, President Xi showed no humanity and no mercy.

If this is how China treats its most famous political prisoner, it is self-evident that the brutality of the Chinese government in repressing its own population is as complete as it is unapologetic. Truly anything can be justified in the name of the greater good.

Yet despite the tragedy that Liu's freedom has come from his death, it is clear today that the Chinese government has lost. Liu's ideas and his dreams will persist, spread, and will, one day, come to fruition. And his courage and his sacrifice for his country will inspire millions of Chinese activists and dissidents to persevere until China has become the multi-party democracy that Liu knew to his core was within its people's grasp.

So what do we do from here? The work is clearly not done, in many different respects.

First and most importantly, the world must rescue Liu Xia. She must be immediately allowed to have open communication with the outside world and her wishes for the burial of her husband and the relocation of herself and her family must be fully honored. Given she is under no legal restriction, this should be easy to achieve.

Second, the world must never forget Liu Xiaobo and what he stood for. I would urge all freedom-loving countries all around the world, starting with the United States, to rename the street in front of their Chinese Embassy "Liu Xiaobo Plaza." The Chinese government is literally erasing him from existence in China. If you type his name in Chinese in the WeChat program online, his name is instantly erased. The Chinese government should never be allowed to forget Liu Xiaobo.

And finally, the best way for the world to honor the legacy of Liu Xiaobo would be to stand in solidarity with the Chinese people's struggle for freedom, democracy, and human rights.

As I noted before, the last time the world heard from Liu was in a statement released by his counsel on December 25, 2009, right after he was sentenced to 11 years imprisonment. Liu said, "I have long been aware that when an independent intellectual stands up to an autocratic state, step one toward freedom is often a step into prison. Now I am taking that step; and true freedom is that much nearer." It is tragic that Liu was only truly free when his soul left his body. But the legacy he left behind will never be forgotten.

Mr. SMITH. Mr. Genser, thank you very much.
Dr. Link.

STATEMENT OF PERRY LINK, PH.D., CHANCELLORIAL CHAIR FOR INNOVATIVE TEACHING, UNIVERSITY OF CALIFORNIA, RIVERSIDE

Mr. LINK. I would like to join my fellow witnesses in congratulating Chairman Smith, Ranking Member Bass, Representative Suozzi, and everyone on this committee, not only for this session, but for the many sessions you have done in the past and I hope will continue to do in the future. They truly are important.

In order to challenge a repressive regime like the one in China today, a regime that demands comprehensive control of society and resorts to extreme brutality if it perceives a threat to itself, a person needs to make a judgment that speaking the truth is more important than personal safety. Dozens of Chinese in recent decades have accepted those stakes, have persisted in speaking honestly in public, and have suffered dire consequences.

Liu Xiaobo stood out within this courageous group because of his truly unusual determination. He went to prison four times, yet none of the punishments deflected him in the slightest from his view of the truth or from his willingness to express it.

Three related events during the years 2008 to 2010 turned him into China's most prominent dissident.

One was his sponsorship of the citizen's manifesto called Charter 08, which is the only public document since the Communist revolution in 1949 that calls for an end to one-party rule.

Second is the 11-year prison sentence that was the consequence of having worked on that charter. And third was the 2010 Nobel Peace Prize, which came as a consequence of the prison sentence. So you can see there is a chain of causality there.

Intellectually, Liu was one of those unusual people who could look at human life from the broadest of perspectives and reason about it from first principles. His keen intellect noticed things that others only look at but don't see. He was deeply erudite on a variety of topics in history and literature, both Eastern and Western, ancient and modern.

His remarkable habit of writing free from fear was so natural and routine that it seemed almost genetic, almost something that he himself could not stop. Most Chinese writers today, including many of the best ones, write with political caution in the backs of their minds and with a shadow hovering over their fingers as they pass across a keyboard. How should I couch things? What topics should I not touch? What indirection should I use?

Liu Xiaobo did none of this. With him, it was all there. What he thought, we got.

The combination of Charter 08 and the Nobel Prize seemed for a time to open an alternative for China, a new alternative. Chinese citizens had long been accustomed to the periodic alternations between more liberal, so-called, and more conservative, so-called, tendencies within Communist rule, as if those limits described how far one could think.

But Charter 08 removed the blinkers and showed that there could be another way to be a modern Chinese. It was hard to find

Chinese people who disagreed with the charter once they read it, and this potential for contagion was clearly the reason why the regime suppressed it.

Today, the severe tightening of controls on Chinese society that has come during the last few years under the rule of Xi Jinping has pushed China in the opposite direction from what the charter stood for, and the question, therefore, arises, is the charter dead? Was the effort in vain?

This question is difficult, but my answer would be no. The movement has been crushed, but its ideas have not been. The government's assiduous, unremitting, and very expensive efforts to repress anything that resembles the ideas in Charter 08 is evidence enough that the men who rule are quite aware of the continuing potential of the ideas to spread.

Liu Xiaobo has been compared to Nelson Mandela, Vaclav Havel, and Aung San Suu Kyi, each of whom who accepted prison as the price for conceiving and pursuing more humane governance in their homelands. But Mandela, Havel, and Suu Kyi all lived to see release from the beastly regimes that repressed them, and Liu Xiaobo did not.

Does this mean his place in history will fall short of theirs? Is success of a movement necessary in order for its leader to be viewed as heroic? Perhaps so.

It may be useful, though, to compare Liu Xiaobo and China's President Xi Jinping for a moment. The two men differ in age by only 2 years. During Mao Zedong's Cultural Revolution both missed school and were banished to remote places. Xi Jinping used the time to begin building a resume that would allow him, by riding the coattails of his elite Communist father, to vie one day for supreme power. Liu Xiaobo used the same time to read on his own and learn to think for himself. One of them mastered the skullduggery and sycophancy that a person needs in order to rise within a closed bureaucracy. The other of them learned to challenge received wisdom of every kind, keeping for himself only the ideas that could pass the test of rigorous independent examination by himself. For one of them, value was measured by power and position. For the other, by moral worth.

Today, after their final standoff, one of them has "won," the other has "lost." But 200 years from now who will remember the names of the tyrants who sent Mandela and Havel and Suu Kyi to jail? Will the glint of Liu Xiaobo's incisive intellect be remembered or the cardboard mediocrity of Xi Jinping's?

I have just a few extra comments on his final days.

Before Liu Xiaobo died of liver cancer in a prison ward in a Shenyang hospital, he asked for safe passage for himself, his wife, and his brother-in-law to go to Germany or the U.S. The two Western governments agreed, but the Chinese Government, saying Liu was already receiving the best possible medical care and was too weak to travel, did not.

Until then Liu had always rejected suggestions that he leave China, primarily because dissidents who leave China lose credibility back home. Moreover, Liu had made it his personal mission to show exactly what happens, right to the last detail, when an independent thinker confronts an authoritarian regime.

We do not know why he changed his position in his last few days, but we can guess that the reasons, and I have two guesses. One is the obvious one, that he was critically ill and transfer abroad might have been the only chance, however slight, to save his life.

Second, and I think this is really the more likely, he knew that his death was imminent and wanted to spend the last of his energies to help his beloved and long-suffering wife Liu Xia, who has been held under house arrest for the last 7 years even though formally charged with nothing and who has had bouts of severe depression.

But if Liu's reasoning cannot be known, and now it cannot be, there can be no doubt whatever about the reasoning of his captors. Their concerns had little to do with medical care one way or the other and much to do with preventing Liu Xiaobo from speaking his mind one last time.

What did he see as he lay dying for a world in which China's beastly dictatorship continues to grow? China's rulers are no doubt relieved to see that the answers to that question are now, with his very life, sealed in eternity.

[The prepared statement of Mr. Link follows:]

Testimony of Perry Link

Chancellorial Chair at the University of California, Riverside

at a hearing on the historic significance of Liu Xiaobo

Subcommittee on Africa, Global Health, Global Human Rights, and International Organizations of the U.S. House Committee of Foreign Affairs

July 14, 2017

Liu Xiaobo's Place in History

In order to challenge a repressive regime like the one in China today—a regime that demands comprehensive control of society and resorts to extreme brutality if it perceives a threat to itself—a person needs to make a judgment that speaking the truth is more important than personal safety. Dozens of Chinese in recent decades have accepted those stakes, have persisted in speaking honestly in public, and have suffered dire consequences.

Liu Xiaobo stood out within this courageous group because of his unflagging determination. He went to prison four times, yet none of these punishments deflected him in the slightest from his view of the truth or from his willingness to express it. Three related events during the years 2008 to 2010 turned him China's most prominent dissident: his sponsorship of the citizens' manifesto called "Charter 08," which is the only public document since the Communist revolution in 1949 that calls for an end to one-Party rule; an eleven-year prison sentence that resulted mainly from the publication of the Charter; and the 2010 Nobel Peace Prize, which came when it did because of the long prison sentence.

Intellectually, Liu was one of those unusual people who can look at human life from the broadest of perspectives and reason about it from first principles. His keen intellect noticed things that others also look at, but do not see. He was deeply erudite on a variety of topics in history and literature, both Eastern and Western, ancient and modern. His remarkable habit of writing free from fear was so natural and routine that it seemed almost genetic, almost something he himself could not stop. Most Chinese writers today, including many of the best, write with political caution in the backs of their minds and with a shadow hovering over their fingers as they pass across a keyboard. How should I couch things? What topics should I not touch? What indirection should I use? Liu Xiaobo did none of this. With him, it was all there. What he thought, he wrote.

The combination of Charter 08 and the Nobel Prize seemed, for a time, to open a new alternative for China. Chinese citizens had long been accustomed to the periodic alternations between "more liberal" and "more conservative" tendencies in Communist rule, as if those described the outer limits within which one could think, but Charter 08 removed blinkers and showed there could be another way to be modern Chinese. It was hard to find Chinese people who disagreed with the Charter once they read it, and this potential for contagion was clearly the regime's reason for suppressing it. Today, as the severe tightening of controls on Chinese society that has come during the last few years under the rule of Xi Jinping has pushed China in the opposite direction from what Charter 08 called for, the question arises. "Is the Charter dead? Was the effort in vain?"

The question is difficult, but my answer would be no. The movement has been crushed but its ideas have not been. The government's assiduous, unremitting and very expensive efforts to repress anything that resembles the ideas in Charter 08 is evidence enough that the men who rule are quite aware of the continuing potential of the ideas to spread.

Liu Xiaobo has been compared to Nelson Mandela, Vaclav Havel, and Aung San Suu Kyi, each of whom accepted prison as the price for conceiving and pursuing more humane governance in their homelands. But Mandela, Havel, and Suu Kyi all lived to see release from the beastly regimes that repressed them, and Liu Xiaobo did not. Does this mean his place in history will fall short of theirs? Is success of a movement necessary in order for its leader to be viewed as heroic?

Perhaps. It may be useful, though, to compare Liu Xiaobo and China's President Xi Jinping. The two differ in age by only two years. During Mao's Cultural Revolution both missed school and were banished to remote places. Xi used the time to begin building a resume that would allow him, by riding the coattails of his elite-Communist father, to vie one day for supreme power; Liu used the time to read on his own and learn to think for himself. One mastered the skullduggery and sycophancy that a person needs into order to rise within a closed bureaucracy; the other learned to challenge received wisdom of every kind, keeping for himself only the ideas that could pass the test of rigorous independent examination. For one of them, value was measured by power and position; for the other, by moral worth. Today, after their final standoff, one has "won," the other "lost". But two hundred years from now, who will remember the names of the tyrants who sent Mandela, Havel, and Suu Kyi to jail? Will the glint of Liu Xiaobo's incisive intellect be remembered, or the cardboard mediocrity of Xi's?

Liu's Final Days

Before Liu Xiaobo died of liver cancer in a prison ward in a Shenyang hospital, he asked for safe passage for himself, his wife, and his brother-in-law to go to Germany or the U.S. The two Western governments agreed, but the Chinese government, saying Liu was already receiving the best possible medical care and was too weak to travel, did not.

Until then Liu had always rejected suggestions that he leave China, primarily because dissidents who leave China lose credibility at home. Moreover, Liu had made it his personal mission to show exactly what happens, right to the last detail, when an independent thinker confronts an authoritarian regime.

We do not know why he changed his position in his last few days, but we can guess at the reasons, and I have two guesses. One is the obvious one: he was critically ill and transfer abroad might have been the only chance, however slight, to save his life. Second—and I think this reason is the more likely—he knew his death was imminent and wanted to spend the last of his energies to help his beloved and long-suffering wife Liu Xia, who has been held under house arrest for the last seven years (even though formally charged with nothing) and who has had bouts with severe depression, to get out of China.

But if Liu's reasoning cannot be known, there can be no doubt about the reasoning of his captors: their concerns had little to do with medical care and much to do with preventing Liu Xiaobo from speaking his mind one last time. What did he see, as he lay dying, for a world in which China's beastly dictatorship continues to grow? China's rulers are no doubt relieved to see that Liu's answers to that question are, with his life itself, now sealed in eternity.

Mr. SMITH. Dr. Link, thank you so very much for that eloquent and heartfelt message.

We are privileged on the subcommittee to be joined by Leader Nancy Pelosi, who has been tenacious in her advocacy for Liu Xiaobo and other dissidents in the People's Republic of China.

I would like to yield such time as you like to consume.

Ms. PELOSI. Thank you very much, Mr. Chairman. It is such a sad day for all of us who were so hopeful that we could have seen an opportunity for medical care to be given to Liu Xiaobo in the last days of his life to extend his life, the life of this great man. I thank you, Mr. Chairman, for your ongoing, consistent, per-sistent advocacy for human rights throughout the world, and par-ticularly in this case in China. You and I have worked on these issues for decades. Your staff said to me, "You are now sitting on the Republican side." When it comes to these issues there is no side. We have always worked in a very strong bipartisan way, and I have always saluted your leadership, as well as our colleague Frank Wolf from Virginia, who was also very relentless.

I have seen Dr. Yang's testimony and Mr. Genser's testimony and heard Dr. Link's beautiful statement, as well. I just wanted to make a statement for the record.

I just was being interviewed over in the Capitol for a statement on this, and what I partially said was: The world grieves the loss of Liu Xiaobo, one of the great moral voices of our time. His clarion call for democracy and human rights in China represented the best hopes of humankind. His courage became a poignant symbol for freedom-loving people across the globe.

Liu Xiaobo's death is a tragedy and a deep affront to the basic notions of justice and human dignity. The role that poor medical care in prison played in his death and the cruelty of confining a dying man in captivity away from his family and friends should disturb us all. His arrest for the so-called crime of putting his polit-ical views into writing is a sobering reminder of China's shameful disregard for basic freedoms.

The world is a bleaker place for this crushing loss, but we must continue to carry forward Liu Xiaobo's legacy. America must honor its moral duty to speak out in defense of the many journalists, human rights lawyers, democracy advocates, and religious freedom advocates unjustly and unfairly lost in jail simply for aspiring to a more free and hopeful future.

If we do not speak out for human rights in China because of com-mercial interest [audio malfunction in hearing room.].

Two weeks ago, I was pleased to join Congressman Chris Smith, co-chair of the Congressional-Executive Commission on China, as the House overwhelmingly passed a bipartisan resolution calling for the unconditional release of both Liu Xiaobo and his wife Liu Xia. We strongly hoped that China would heed the call to free Liu Xia for unjust house arrest and will allow her to travel wherever she may choose.

I just want to join Dr. Link in his comments about Liu Xia. Reading from Liu Xiaobo's Nobel lecture in absentia on December 10, 2010, he said in this: "If I may be permitted to say so, the most fortunate experience of these past 20 years has been the selfless love I have received from my wife Liu Xia. She could not be present as observer in the court today," he was talking about the court. "But I want to say to you, my dear, that I firmly believe your love for me will remain the same as it has always been."

More things, but, "Your love is the sunlight that leaps over high walls and penetrates the iron bars of my prison window, stroking every inch of my skin, warming every cell of my body, allowing me to always keep peace, openness, and brightness in my heart. Even if I were crushed into powder I would still use my ashes to embrace you."

I think that he has given us our direction. We must work very hard to protect Liu Xia, hopefully to bring her and brother-in-law of Liu Xiaobo out of China. I will take my guidance from Chairman Smith. We talked about a number of ways to honor the memory of Liu Xiaobo and to honor his love of his wife.

I am particularly happy that Congresswoman Karen Bass is with us today. She is a person who respects the dignity and worth of every person. She works hard for children in our own country and is a supporter of the dignity and worth of people throughout the world.

Thank you, Congresswoman Bass, for making this a priority for us.

And, again, under your leadership, Mr. Chairman, you will give me some guidance as to what you think the best path is to go, but I will close by saying: May Liu Xiaobo life and legacy continue to inspire all who strive for justice and democracy. May his memory be a blessing to us all. And may his family take some solace in knowing that the whole world mourns with them.

And, Dr. Link, I don't think it is going to take 200 years. I think right now and very soon the contribution, the legacy of Liu Xiaobo will certainly eclipse the authoritarians of China.

With that, I thank the chairman and yield back.

Mr. SMITH. Leader Pelosi, thank you very much for your eloquent——

Ms. PELOSI. I am honored that the chairman——

Mr. SMITH. And we are joined by the full committee chairman, the distinguished Ed Royce.

Mr. ROYCE. Well, thank you, Mr. Chairman, very much, and Leader Pelosi.

It is a sad day. Yesterday was a very sad day. A sad day for human rights. I was deeply saddened to learn of Nobel Prize Laureate Liu Xiaobo's tragic passing. I think the world mourns. Our thoughts are with his loved ones, especially his widow, Liu Xia, who has been under house arrest now since 2010.

Liu was a prolific writer. He was an academic. He dedicated his life to giving voice to the oppressed. And he did this by calling for his government to grant more freedom to the Chinese people.

He was imprisoned multiple times, and he was imprisoned for his peaceful protests for human rights and for democracy in China. It happened first during Tiananmen Square in 1989 and later for releasing the Charter 08 manifesto in 2009, which articulated the need for reforms in China. Those reforms, it was his intent, would achieve the rule of law, would achieve freedom of press and speech and religion.

He was an inspiration to all of us. Liu's efforts were not in vain. His sacrifice and death while in the custody of the Chinese Government, while serving an unjustified 11-year prison sentence, has shined a light on the sad state of human rights in China.

As we take stock of these sad events, we should remember that there are prisoners of conscience in China and around the world who continue to need our support. Let us be part of his legacy. May the bravery of Liu Xiaobo inspire us to seek their freedom also.

And thank you again, Mr. Chairman.

Mr. SMITH. Thank you, Chairman Royce.

And, again, thank you, Leader Pelosi. We were together in Oslo.

Ms. PELOSI. What an honor.

Mr. SMITH. And what an honor. And what a heartbreak this is. Hopefully, Liu Xiaobo's death will be a global pivot to human rights in China, and we certainly have to do our part in doing that.

Mr. Suozzi.

Mr. SUOZZI. Thank you, Mr. Chairman. I know we are very rushed for time because we have to go over for votes.

But I just wanted to say, Dr. Yang, my condolences to you.

Mr. Genser and Dr. Link, thank you so much for your life's work and for your testimony, as well.

It is hard to imagine when we are in this air-conditioned room that is so august and in this setting to think of the suffering that went on in his life and now goes on in his wife's life and in so many other people's lives, from cancer to depression and heart attacks and suffering. And this is going on all over the world right now in people who are trying to fight for human rights and fight for human dignity throughout the world.

And his life is such an inspiration to me and I know to so many other others, and we are so grateful to all of you for helping to bring notice to this important message.

You know, China right now is trying to participate in the modern world through its economy. But economic improvement is not a substitute for respect for human dignity and human rights.

And I want the chairman to know and the ranking member to know and the leader to know that I will do everything I can to work with them to support efforts to make sure that this life was not a life in vain.

So thank you so much for everything that you do.

[Speaking foreign language.]

Mr. SMITH. Thank you.

We will take a brief recess. We have votes on the floor. It is actually on zero, so we are going to have to run, but we will be right back.

[Recess.]

Mr. SMITH. The subcommittee will resume its sitting.

And, Dr. Yang, I know you do have to go to the funeral of your brother-in-law. And, again, my greatest sympathies to you and your family. But, please.

Mr. YANG. I have a few further points to make, then I can leave. Mr. Chairman, Liu Xiaobo represents the best of what China can be, in death as well as in life. He possesses a moral authority that his persecutors can only envy. His legacy of love, just as in courage, will surely far outlive the deeds of those who persecuted him.

Liu Xiaobo was a major leader of the 1989 democracy movement. He shouldered moral and political responsibility after Tiananmen Square, continued to fight inside China for its constitutional democracy while many left the country and even left the movement. He shared the suffering of his compatriots and made great sacrifices for them. He is a saint. His spirit will be an uplifting and unifying force that will inspire more people of China to fight to realize his dream, indeed the common dream of Chinese people.

To the world, he represents the universal values that all democracies embrace and the unwavering struggle of unfree people for freedom. Liu Xiaobo is a representative of ideas that resonate with millions of people all over the world.

But it is a sad and disturbing fact that many leaders of the free world, who themselves hold democracy and human rights in high regard, have been less willing to stand up for those rights for the benefit of others. If this became a widely accepted fashion and continued, the democratic way and the security of the free people would eventually be in jeopardy.

Today I cannot help asking, what kind of a government would refuse to grant the final wish of such a peaceful, kind of man as Liu Xiaobo, a man who sincerely believes that he has no enemies, to die as a free man, to die with dignity? What kind of a government would not even allow him the last moment of being with his beloved wife without surveillance?

This is a totally morally bankrupted regime. Dealing with such a regime, one must have moral clarity. There is a lot of talking about engaging with China, yes, no one can avoid engaging with China. But democracies must engage China comprehensively. Democracies must engage this brutal face of this regime and must not look the other way when human rights tragedies take place. The Chinese Government can never be considered a true trusted peer on the global stage until they address their egregious human rights violations.

The tragic passing of Liu Xiaobo gives us a stronger sense of urgency to help other dissidents. I am afraid that more human rights activists will languish and disappear in China's prisons: Wang Bingzhang, Hu Shigen, Zhu Yufu, Ilham Tohti, Tashi Wangchuk, Wang Quanzhang, Jiang Tianyong, Tang Jingling, Wu Gan, Guo Feixiong, Liu Xianbin, Chen Wei, Zhang Haitao, the list goes on. If American advocacy for human rights and justice is to mean anything at all, the U.S. Government must do more to support these political prisoners and to hold accountable the government and the individuals who so brazenly abuse their fundamental rights.

We all hoped that Liu Xiaobo would one day complete his unjust prison sentence and then have more time to share his passion and energy for human rights and dignity; and also, perhaps, one day to have time to enjoy for himself the fruits of freedom. But instead he is gone.

To close, I want to share with you the beautiful words of Martin Luther King, Jr., which he delivered in a speech in Memphis, Tennessee, on the evening before his own death:

Well, I don't know what will happen now. We have got some difficult days ahead. But it really does not matter with me now, because I have been to the mountaintop and I don't mind.

Like anybody, I would like to live a long life. Longevity has its place. But I am not concerned about that now. I just want to do God's will. And he has allowed me to go up to the mountain. And I have looked over, and I have seen the promised land. I may not get there with you. But I want you to know tonight that we, as a people, will get to the promised land.

Thank you.

Mr. SMITH. Dr. Yang, thank you for your passion and precision and how we present. It is just couldn't be clearer the stark difference between the gross evil of what is done by the leadership of the PRC and a man of light of Liu Xiaobo's character.

So thank you for your—all three of you—thank you for bearing witness to the noble truth of this man and what he stood for.

I note again, Dr. Yang, in your testimony you pointed out that the denial of medical care led to Liu Xiaobo's liver cancer, and it was at its core a disguised death sentence. To not treat, certainly no early detection, and as you point out in your testimony, as far as back as 2010 Liu Xiaobo was suspected of suffering from hepatitis B.

His lawyers—and, Mr. Genser, you spoke about this many times—petitioned the government and kept asking to grant him A medical parole to get the healthcare, the health attention that he needed rather than languishing in a horrific jail cell.

I think the other story that needs to be told by the media globally is this whole death sentence. It wasn't like he got Johns Hopkins-like medical care or Sloan Kettering-grade medical care. He was ignored. The evidence clearly suggests that they did nothing or very little. And to deny his request to go to Germany or to here to get the kind of care he needs and to turn that down shows a barbarity that just needs to be confronted aggressively.

Like I said earlier, I think this needs to be the pivot to human rights in his legacy, of course, but because there are so many others still suffering horribly in laogai and throughout the Chinese concentration camp system.

And when Xi Jinping goes to Davos and talks about transparency and openness, it is a cruel joke. And I am glad that the administration did put China on Tier 3 for its egregious abuses with regards to sex and labor trafficking. Magnitsky needs to be full throttled in its implementation to hold individuals to account.

The International Religious Freedom Act, which has China as a country of particular concern, or CPC country, carries with it at least 18 prescribed sanctions that can be very, very potent if utilized. They have not been. There has to be a response to this the likes of which we have never seen before.

As you said so eloquently, Dr. Yang, a disguised death sentence. For what? For peacefully asking for fundamental freedoms and human rights.

So if any of you would like to comment on this lack of medical attention, which is appalling, please do. And I do have some other questions. But any other points you would like to make, as well, we would like to receive.

Mr. YANG. Mr. Chairman, I have to leave right now.

Mr. GENSER. I do want to build on Global Magnitsky. And my view is—and I will work on this myself—is I would like to put together a comprehensive list of everybody who was responsible for Liu Xiaobo's arrest, trial, imprisonment, and care, or lack thereof, from the prosecutor, to the judge, to the person who ran his prison, to the hospital where he died.

It seems to me that we can put together a list of a dozen or 15 names of people that are directly responsible for what happened to him. And that should be among a number of different things that are done to send a very clear message about where the United States stands in regards to those who are actually responsible.

There will be no justice and accountability, of course, for anybody in China. But there needs to be some measure of justice and accountability for Liu Xiaobo as part of his legacy and to send a very clear signal about there being consequences to decisions that are being made at all levels of government in China. So that is what I would just have to say on Global Magnitsky.

Mr. LINK. It is worth noting, I think, that the pattern of having political prisoners die in prison in China is a pattern. It is not just that Liu Xiaobo was the first one. A few years ago a woman named Cao Shunli, who is not nearly as famous as he is, was ground to death. She disappeared about September 15 on her way to go to Geneva for a report on human rights in China. The police took her into prison. And she was released 6 months later in a coma, given to her family after it was clear that she would not live but not wanting her to die in prison because the regime is afraid of that black eye on its record.

I would like to make another point, though, as we remember this man. I think it is important that we—and by "we," I mean the whole world—recognize him as a world-class person, not just a China person. We China scholars have the problem, I think, of thinking that he speaks for China, and he is talking about Chinese human rights, and we are dealing with the Chinese Government. And all of that is true. But he speaks to the whole world.

In my statement a moment ago, I referred to Mandela and Havel and Aung San Suu Kyi, all of whom are viewed as world-class upholders of freedom and human rights, and he should be too.

I noticed on the PBS television program that announced his death last night, I was waiting to see which China scholar would come on and talk about it. But they didn't have a China scholar. They had a man from India who represented Amnesty International, and I thought that was wonderful. Because the point is he speaks for all of humanity, not just Chinese humanity.

And in that connection, I think it is good that this subcommittee is on Africa, Global Health, Global Human Rights, and International Organizations. That is a very good step toward saying what Liu Xiaobo stood for is universal human rights, not just China.

Mr. SMITH. Let me ask you, Dr. Link. You have testified before, and I appreciate your testimony you have provided us on the whole university, the 12 campuses—like NYU, for example, Kean College—in China, on Mainland China, and then all the Confucius centers?

Has there been any response over the last 2 weeks. We passed a resolution—I authored it, it was cosponsored by Leader Pelosi, so it was totally and absolutely bipartisan, and it passed unanimously in the House 2 weeks ago—calling for Liu Xiaobo and his wife and family to be able to come here or wherever they would like to go for medical treatment.

Have we heard anything on those campuses or at the Confucius centers about the life and the tremendous legacy and the work of Liu Xiaobo.

Mr. LINK. The Confucius centers are on living, breathing, U.S. campuses. So it is certain that some people on those campuses notice these things and support them.

I haven't done a survey of what the Confucius Institute's leaders themselves have done, but I feel very confident in saying, no, they wouldn't touch it with a 10-foot pole. They get money from the Hanban in China. And without it being in written form, know that there are certain things you just don't do. You don't entertain the Dalai Lama or Liu Xiaobo or the Falun Gong problem or Tibet or Xinjao or the Beijing massacre. There is a list of about two dozen utterly untouchable topics that Confucius Institutes just don't observe.

Mr. SMITH. My hope is—and we will, as the Congressional-Executive Commission on China, which I also co-chair with Marco Rubio—I think it would be very timely for us to write them and ask them to raise the issue of Liu Xiaobo's widow, Liu Xia. You know, NYU Shanghai campus, and I did speak there a little over a year ago, on human rights. And, of course, Liu Xiaobo was one of the first things I said there.

But they have, I think, an obligation, I would say a moral duty to speak out, because they tell us that they have academic freedom and the ability to speak in an unfettered way. And you are right. There are economic interests intertwined. But the hope would be that America's voice—and I would say not just America, a universally important, universally recognized human rights voice needs to be articulated now.

There needs to be a pivot to human rights. The old days have to be over of just thinking that backdoor diplomacy and mentioning it, you know, under your breath is going to work. It is not going to work. It has not worked.

We had a number of women testify here before our subcommittee just recently, all the wives of human rights lawyers who have been detained pursuant to that crackdown by Xi Jinping. And to hear them tell their stories about, you know, their husbands, and them, because they suffer equally. The idealism is just breathtaking. And yet they are in prison.

Same way with the five daughters hearing that we had of all of those young Chinese daughters who couldn't even get a meeting with President Obama. And they pleaded with us to tell him, please let us talk to him face-to-face, he has two daughters, he will understand. They never got the meeting. And they were articulate and they were daughters that just spoke out so articulately and bravely on behalf of their dads who are suffering like Gao Zhisheng and others.

So I think that is something we need to do, is to get at least these U.S. universities, which should or used to be beacons of academic freedom and human rights and inquiry, to raise the issue of Liu Xiaobo's widow, and the work and legacy of Liu Xiaobo himself, and Charter 08, the great manifesto.

Mr. LINK. I think it is a brilliant idea to have you or others in the Congress write to all of the American campuses, especially the prestigious ones who have accepted Confucius Institutes, first asking the question, saying, a Nobel Peace Prize winner has died in police custody in China, surely, this is a topic worth note. What has your institute done about it? And then go on to ask the question, what are your plans for helping the wife?

Mr. SMITH. Thank you, Dr. Link.

Mr. Garrett.

Mr. GARRETT. Thank you, Mr. Chairman.

And thank you for convening this meeting.

And my apologies, candidly, to our guests. The timing is not the best. But, obviously, it coincides with this tragic loss of the life of a vocal leader for human rights around the world.

It strikes me that the balance that the United States maintains with China is an interesting one, that we might be to a greater extent than perhaps in any era in recent history rivals. And yet we are arguably codependent upon one another economically and globally.

The paramount interest of our office, and I think my constituents, based on my listening, is that there would be peace and stability and that there would be a fundamental right to an opportunity extended to people within the Fifth District of Virginia, the United States, and, candidly, globally. And pardon me if I don't do service to Liu Xiaobo's name.

But when a person of this magnitude exercises the moral courage which we have witnessed in this country through the statements and actions of people like Patrick Henry and Martin Luther King, Barbara Johns and Abraham Lincoln, it is, indeed, as you say, something that should be taken note of by the world. While folks of my political ilk might sometimes find fault with some of the selections of the Nobel Committee, I think they could have found no more appropriate recipient than Liu Xiaobo.

And one of the things that I have crusaded for as a member of the statehouse and now the Congress is a greater awareness by Americans of who Barbara Johns was. She was a 16-year-old girl who led a student walkout in Farmville, Virginia, in the early 1950s, which really sparked the civil rights movement in Virginia, and did so at the imperilment of her own life, and that of others, and did so at a time when at a similar age I was concerned with popping zits and whether or not I could get a prom date.

And so sometimes I wonder what we do well here, what we can accomplish here. But, to this end, I would say, Congressman Smith, gentlemen, folks in the room, that the more people we can get to go to Google and type in Liu Xiaobo's name and understand what he did in the face of the odds in which he did it, the more Liu Xiaobos there will be.

I guess, to the extent that we can help, I commend you on raising the awareness and teaching about folks who we might not agree with on every single piece of subject matter, but who stand for fundamental truths that no one who is an America can deny, and that is that all people are created equal and endowed by their Creator with certain rights.

And so I suppose I will take my time here to query both of you. What, again, within the purview of the legislative branch of the United States Federal Government we can do to ensure that his legacy doesn't die with his physical body, to insist that an important trade partner and member of the world community, China, understands that we give a damn—pardon me—and to encourage greater freedom and opportunity across the globe, and do so wherever practical and possible without bombs and bullets and missiles and rockets, but brave men and women who are willing to stand up in the face of potential imprisonment or worse.

So I would offer first Mr. Genser the floor for suggestions. What can we do within the purview of Article I to help perpetuate the legacy of this great leader to convey to our Chinese partners that we care, that we will not sit by idly as members of, say, for example, the Falun Gong, are imprisoned on the eve of what was supposed to be a meeting with U.S. leadership? What can we do to abate my fear that when spouses of imprisoned dissidents show up before this committee they have only made their family's circumstance worse?

Mr. GENSER. Thanks, Congressman Garrett, for your remarks, with which I fully agree, and your commitment to human rights, as well. Let me just mention a couple of things that I think are important that the Congress could be particularly involved in helping. The first, of course, and most importantly, is to help get Liu Xia and her brother out of China as rapidly as possible. We need to re-store access to them and then confirm their wishes and get them out. And that should be a top priority.

And I think that pressure by having this hearing today, pressure by moving a bill that is focused on Liu Xia and her brother, we have also been talking about a private Member's bill that would give them legal permanent resident status immediately upon arriving in the United States, these are things that Congress can do. So that would be number one.

Number two, Liu Xiaobo Plaza, renaming the street in front of the Chinese Embassy for Liu Xiaobo, I think, is a way that the United States and governments all over the world—I am sure, we will be campaigning for this—for all countries in the world to rename the streets in front of the Chinese Embassy Liu Xiaobo Plaza. This is something that, obviously, has to go through the Congress, and then go to the President for signature.

Number three, justice and accountability. And I was just mentioning, as well, having a list of those responsible for Liu Xiaobo and Liu Xia's deaths, to have the Congress advocating to have them sanctioned under Global Magnitsky and to make clear that this is why they are being sanctioned.

And then let me just step back broadly and make a final point, which is something that—I have spent my career as a human rights lawyer fighting for the freedom of prisoners of conscience. I spent 5 years Aung San Suu Kyi's international counsel. I have represented more than 40 prisoners of conscience over my career and founded Freedom Now, my NGO, on whose board I sit, which has a full-time staff in Washington and London to work on these cases.

One of the things I think the U.S. needs to do more directly, and I think the Congress could play a key role in a legislative context, is to focus our foreign policy on the world's prisoners of conscience. Because it seems to me that we have annual human rights reports, and that is really good, and prisoners of conscience are kind of a narrow piece of it, but a more focused set of activities for the United States to focus on prisoners of conscience.

Because what we have found historically—and we were talking about a lot of different, obviously, names, people like Havel, people like Mandela—is that the prisoners of conscience of today are the leaders of their countries tomorrow, and that for the United States to stand in solidarity with homegrown pro-democracy activists, not the United States imposing our values or our form of government onto others, but embracing those that within their own countries see the value of democracy, the value of human freedom, and to systematically as part of our foreign policy and engaging with every country in the world, any country that is persecuting prisoners of conscience, our engagement with that country, not just from the State Department or the National Security Council, but from every agency, can be focused on a list of names that would be raised, focused on training Foreign Service Officers to do these kinds of things, focused on reporting requirements for the State Department about what is being done to help these people.

What is interesting is that if you look at the case of Natan Sharansky, who of course was a Soviet dissident, whose wife, Avital, met with President Reagan, a mentor of mine in my career, Irwin Cotler, was his counsel and had a chance to talk to Gorbachev about, "Why did you release Natan Sharansky?"

And what Gorbachev said was really telling, and I think really, really important, which was to say that, "Well, I didn't know who this guy Natan Sharansky was until I was"—many years before he became the President of the Soviet Union he was Minister of Agriculture. And he came to the United States on some kind of agricultural exchange and discussion about, well, agricultural issues. And, yet, on the U.S. side, our Agriculture Secretary raised to him Natan Sharansky's name in a meeting about agriculture.

And one of the first things he did when he became President, he told my friend and mentor, Irwin Cotler, was to ask the secret police, the KGB, for the file of Natan Sharansky, because he had heard about this in many meetings with U.S. Government officials over and over and over again. And it was like, why is the Agriculture Secretary doing this? And he looked at the file and he was like, well, this makes no sense, why is this guy in jail? And ultimately he was released.

And so, to me, that is an important lesson for the United States, that prisoners of conscience and helping people of this sort isn't just the responsibility of some narrow Assistant Secretary for Democracy, Labor, and Human Rights to be raising, but that it has to be part and parcel and central to U.S. foreign policy as a strategic tactic to be regularly deployed to try to advance human freedom around the world.

So let me conclude with that.

Mr. GARRETT. So to some degree the Sharansky case was almost a "ye have not because ye ask not."

Mr. GENSER. Right.

Mr. GARRETT. One thing that I probably unintelligently voiced my frustration with, and I have only been here for a short time, is that I don't feel that we have synergy between the executive and the legislative as it relates to working together. We have worked on the release of some prisoners of conscience, particularly in the southern Nuba Mountain regions of the Republic of Sudan, and I almost feel like the State Department wants to know why I care. God bless the good men and women there, but we should be working together to advance the same goals. And wherever any human being is held prisoner based on beliefs, unless those beliefs advocate violence against other humans, why can't we all agree on that, right?

So thank you immensely, and I would love to speak to you briefly after the hearing about what you do, because I think we might be able to help to the same, I think, admirable goal.

The only thing that I have been able to do in 6 months here that I can take pride in and take to my grave is help affect the release of individuals held because of their beliefs, right? It is hard to pass a bill. But when you tell somebody the United States of America is looking and cares about some formerly nameless individual in prison because of their faith or their actions of humanity toward another and something happens, then you go, maybe this is all worth it. Thanks for what you do.

Dr. Link, what else, within the context of the legislative role of the Article I constitutional underpinnings of this body should we be doing that we are not doing? And, by the way, I texted my legislative director during your comments to get us on the bill that is out there as it relates to the plaza, the Liu Xiaobo Plaza.

Mr. LINK. Let me add my voice to the chorus that says that the Liu Xiaobo Plaza is a great idea. I really strongly endorse that, and also endorse what my colleague Jared Genser said in some more detail about focus of foreign policy on prisoners of conscience.

I think it is often perceived that we do that because it makes us feel better. And that is good. We should feel better. It is right to do the right thing and we are better people for doing it. But what he has pointed out is that it is also an investment in practical terms in a better world, because these people that we are helping emerge—Havel did, Mandela did, Aung San Suu Kyi did, Liu Xiaobo can't, but there are more—it is a good investment from a practical point of view.

I would add a third, which Jared sort of mentioned, but I would put it this way, and that is the bully pulpit is a good thing to use. It sounds like we are just pontificating, preaching and so on, and that there might be backlash. But I think that is not right. Even the leaders, even the oppressors in China, at another level, know that democracy and human rights are a good thing. Watch the way they put the word democracy in their own rhetoric. Stalin, Lenin, said they had democratic centralism. Mao Zedong said it was democratic centralism. North Korea, the most repugnant state on the face of the globe today, calls itself the Democratic People's Republic of Korea.

There is a two-leveledness in the psychology of the oppressors. They want it both ways. On the surface, okay, the West is bad, the West's values are not universal, and they are oppressing us, and so on. But I am going to send my daughter to Harvard. Xi Jinping's daughter went there. Send them money.

I am from California. The Los Angeles area is full of communities that are built on money—probably corrupt money—shipped from China that the privileged elite in China wants to ship abroad. They send their kids to go to U.S. schools more and more and more.

So what does this say? Does this say that they hate Western values? No. It is a rivalrous feeling. And at one level they say, we are all against you. But at another level, we are sending our children and our money to your country for safekeeping.

So that gives us a platform on which to say, without apology, democracy, freedom, human rights are good things. And they may say on the surface, no, no, no, no, no, that is Western imperialism. Underneath, they know it is not. A lot of them know it is not.

Therefore, I think what I have just called the bully pulpit, when our officials go to the G20 meetings, when they go to the United Nations, or through VOA and Radio Free Asia, don't be embarrassed to put our values out there. There is more to them than the tyrants in China want to admit.

Mr. GARRETT. Thank you, Dr. Link.

I would beg the chairman's indulgence for another question that is tangentially related and not directly related. But your comments have got the wheels turning a little bit.

There is some call from various sectors to, in order to exert pressure on the Chinese to exert pressure on North Korea, consider rolling back admissions of Chinese students to U.S. universities.

My immediate reaction is that we don't have a Sisi in Egypt if there is not a period of learning and experiencing American culture, that we don't have any number of leaders abroad who have turned out to be pretty good allies if they hadn't spent time here in the United States. So there is back-end value to having the children, even of the Chinese ruling class, in American institutions.

Having said that, the secondary argument is there is a rivalry, there is a need for engineers and software developers and expertise, and there is a competitive nature to it whether we like it or not. And our institutions are producing the young women and men who are beating us at our own game, if you will.

I would love your opinion on the idea that somehow denying access to our universities might advance goals as it relates to human rights and stability and safety on the Korean Peninsula and as it relates to geopolitical stability and security, which might manifest itself differently based on the regions from which our excellent young students might matriculate. This is an opinion question. There are no wrong answers.

Mr. LINK. As a broad principle, I would say that it is good for us to take the children of anybody if they are smart enough to get through the universities and do well, and that the long-range effect of a U.S. education on the children of the Chinese elite is a good thing. And I work in the university.

I make certain exceptions for that though. About a week ago a Wall Street Journal columnist named Bill McGurn called me up, and he asked me what I thought of targeting the offspring of the super elite in China and denying them visas to come to Harvard and Stanford and Chicago as a method of getting leverage for China to cooperate on North Korea. And I said, I think that is a good idea.

So there is an exception there to my broader principle. And I would just say I make that exception because it is well known that we have no good options on North Korea. And if you bomb and attack, that is going to wreak havoc. It is going to destroy the city of Seoul. If you just do what we have done for the last three decades, which is to cross your fingers and hope for the best, that is not working either.

What can we do? China, of course, can play a key role. That would be the way to really bring pressure on the North Korean regime. But China won't. I think the Chinese leadership likes their position of being able to waffle and have us constantly begging them to help, and they say they will, but then they don't, and so on. That is their endgame. They like that.

So when Bill McGurn asked me is this a way to get the top leaders' attention in a very personal way, I said yes. And I would make that exception.

Mr. GARRETT. Thank you.

And, Mr. Genser, if you have any comments to that, I would welcome them. I don't want to freeze you out here.

Mr. GENSER. I agree with Perry on this. I think as a strategic question overall, I think the more that we can expose foreigners to U.S. universities the more that our system of government, the system, the free market, our values, will be transmitted.

But you look at certain countries in the world and their leaders send their kids to the United States, and you may have a different take on it. So, for example, let's take Iran. It was reported in the media about 1 year, 1½ years ago, that the woman who was actually the spokesperson for the students who took the U.S. Embassy in 1979, Masoumeh Ebtekar, who was referred to as Mary back then as the spokeswoman, her son is getting his Ph.D. in California. And she is the sitting Vice President of Iran and the head of their EPA and has been an unrepentant person with respect to everything relating to the United States and including her role in taking American hostages.

Do I think it is a good idea to allow someone like that to have their child educated in the United States? Not really. My view is that while ordinarily I would never want to punish a child for the sins of his or her father or mother, in a case like that, where the person is a sitting senior leader and is an unrepentant hostage taker, I don't think that we should be opening up our borders freely to people like that.

And I would note, as well, that among my other clients are Siamak and Baquer Namazi, two American citizen hostages in Iran, two of four currently. And so Iran isn't just historically having taken hostages, but it is doing so today. And the current Government of Iran, and particularly the Revolutionary Guard Corps, are responsible for that.

So it does seem to me that one needs to be smart about this and not just go with a big hammer and say, well, let's just not let people in. But I think that strategically the United States can definitely use access to our university system to send targeted messages in the right way and in the right time.

Mr. GARRETT. So, Mr. Chairman, I will wrap up.

So, in conclusion, I would ask the yes-or-no question, the succinct summary of what you said is, if we target specific individuals and paint with a very narrow brush, that there can be an effective outcome. If we paint with a broad brush and essentially say, we are not going to have students from country X, it is probably deleterious to our long-term desires.

Mr. GENSER. Yes.

Mr. LINK. Correct.

Mr. GARRETT. Thank you guys immensely. And, again, Mr. Genser, if you will stick around for a little bit, I would be grateful.

Mr. SMITH. Thank you very much, Mr. Garrett. And I will just conclude and then ask if you have any final statements that you would like to make before we end the hearing.

Just for the record, Senator Cruz's bill to rename International Drive Liu Xiaobo Plaza has been hotlined in the Senate. Unfortunately, it has a couple of holds on it, and that is the way the Senate works. One member can hold up a bill. But it is being actively pursued there.

And Mark Meadows, a member of our subcommittee, has introduced H.R. 2537 to rename Liu Xiaobo Plaza. And our hope is as soon as that can get approved, the better. And I am very proud to be one of the cosponsors, following his lead on that.

Just one brief point about a whole-of-government approach. We recently enacted the Frank Wolf International Religious Freedom Act, and one of the main parts of that legislation was to have a whole-of-government approach so that you don't get a human rights dialogue that becomes a means unto an end, where it is like a cul-de-sac, you know, everyone talks, everybody leaves, there is no connection to anything else.

We need the U.S. Trade Representative, we need people in the military, particularly when there is a government-to-government contact of some kind, to almost, as you pointed out with the Agriculture Secretary and Natan Sharansky, or agriculture officials, that they realize that every time they turn around a group of noble dissidents are being named as being high priority to the United States. When you don't do that, that speaks volumes as well.

So that Religious Freedom Act also has prisoners lists by country, which I think has been long overlooked. Some of the dissidents in the political sphere get good mention by the Bureau of Democracy, Human Rights, and Labor, which is good. But, again, it often stops there.

So we need this whole-of-government approach so that everyone—and that would go for Members of Congress as well, that when we travel we don't go to China and fail to bring up—particularly if you meet with a leader—the names, and the more specific, the better.

I will never forget Frank Wolf and I met with Li Peng back in the 1990s. And our delegation, he and I, and our staff, were merged with a trade delegation. Thankfully, we got the seats closest to Li Peng, Premier, and we raised the issues specifically of names, Tiananmen Square names, went through religious freedom, forced abortion. We laid out a human rights case. He sat there almost bewildered. Who let these two guys in? But the whole discussion was about that.

The next day he met with another group from America, and he launched into a tirade about democracy and how they protect democracy, and he was all-on defensive mode, because they have much to be ashamed of.

These are willful acts they have taken. What they did to Liu Xiaobo, what they continue to do to his wife, is by design, not by default. And so we need to hold them to account. And my hope is that this new administration will do a whole-of-government approach.

And, lastly, I learned a lesson from Wei Jingsheng when he was briefly let out of prison to procure the 2000 Olympics for China. They eventually got it in 2008, but they wanted it in 2000. A high value political prisoner, father of the Democracy Wall movement who spent 18 years in prison. He went back in after we met and had dinner together—not right away, but when they didn't get the 2000 Olympics.

He said, everybody in America and in policymaking around the world need to understand that when you kowtow they beat us more in the prison. It follows right through into the prison cell itself, and those who administer torture and other horrible misdeeds against prisoners.

When you are tough, predictable, look them in the eyes and say, we know what you are doing, we know what you have been doing to Liu Xiaobo all these years, and you bring it up every time, they beat us less and they treat us better. And people do get out of prison. They often go on parole, but they are at least home.

And so, again, this pivot to human rights in China that the horrific death, death sentence of Liu Xiaobo, is now that the Western governments led by the United States need to say, now we are all in, in the legacy and in the great pioneering work that was done by Liu Xiaobo.

So if you would like to conclude, or if Mr. Garrett wants to conclude with any statement, I would just yield to my friends at the witness table.

Mr. LINK. I will tell one anecdote to reinforce the point you just made. My wife is Chinese, and she was a protester in the 1989 events and was sent to a labor camp for 3 years. And she had also studied law. And she looked up the law, and it says in the law of the labor camps that you can labor only 8 hours a day and they were having to labor 14 hours a day. So she said, no, I am only going to do 8 hours a day.

And so the prison authorities organized a group of other prisoners to beat her. And they did. And this was terrible. She suffered beatings.

She snuck out a note via another prisoner who was leaving to her mother. Her mother told Human Rights Watch in New York.

Human Rights Watch publicized her case, and immediately the beatings stopped, and she only had to work 8 hours a day.

Mr. GENSER. I will end with an anecdote that is a tragic anecdote, but a reason, I think, for further motivation for us to proceed full force on all of these issues, which is that over the years I have been in touch with many human rights lawyers in China and worked with many of them as well. And obviously I can't provide any names here publicly. But there have been a number of human rights lawyers I know that have been vigorously interrogated by Chinese authorities, beaten and treated very badly, some of whom, of course, have been sent to prison, others not.

But, unfortunately, Liu Xiaobo's name has been invoked by the torturers in torturing individual people in China in recent years. And this is when they are trying to persuade a human rights lawyer who maybe hasn't been as aggressive yet, as somebody like a Gao Zhisheng, where as they are beating them, they say, this is pointless, you are never going to succeed standing up to the one-party system.

And look at the case of Liu Xiaobo, the world's only imprisoned Nobel Peace Prize laureate, and we are holding his wife with impunity, right? The world knows who he is and can't do anything about it. What hope do you have of standing up to our Government? You should just give up right now.

And this is the refrain that the torturers use as they torture people, or certain people, in China. And to me this is both unsurprising and equally horrific at the same time. But this only reaffirms why we need to do everything humanly possible to keep Liu Xiaobo's memory alive and to stand in solidarity with the prisoners of conscience whose names Yang Jianli was mentioning earlier, as well as the countless hundreds, thousands, tens of thousands of others we don't really even know that are suffering.

We can't let the anonymous prisoner of conscience be forgotten in China because they will do whatever they would like to them. And I think that the case of Liu Xiaobo will also be remembered, I think in the best sense, for being, hopefully, a line in the sand where the international community is able to say to China, enough, enough.

We are mutually interdependent, as I think Congressman Garrett was saying, on trade, on intellectual property, on North Korea, around all the things we have to work on. And China can't afford to walk away from its relationship with the United States because it gets angry with the United States for raising human rights. It isn't going to happen under any circumstance. And they are not going to dump our trillion dollars-plus of Treasuries either, because they are smart and they do not want to lose a lot of money.

So they are forced to deal with us on human rights. And why the international community has engaged in so much self-censorship, to me, boggles my mind.

I also agree—I just want to conclude by noting what Chairman Smith was saying about these human rights dialogues. I have always joked that, based on friends of mine who have been on them on the U.S. side, and I have heard stories about how they go, that these actually aren't human rights dialogues. They are really human rights sequential monologues.

And maybe the Congress could force the administration to call them that, right? We are no longer going to have human rights dialogues with China. We are going to require them to be publicly labeled human rights sequential monologues if we are going to keep doing them. Because it is not like either side is giving anything. And the Chinese side, especially, is just giving speeches that are prepared and aren't able to do anything at all.

So I also, as well, want to conclude by thanking particularly Chairman Smith. I am obviously also grateful for Mr. Garrett, but particularly Chairman Smith for your commitment over decades on China human rights. You have just been indefatigable, relentless, and are such an extraordinary champion here in the Congress on China rights issues, along with Leader Pelosi and others.

But the fact that this subcommittee is so focused on China and so focused on human rights more broadly, I don't know what we would do without you, Mr. Chairman, being here and your leadership. And so it is always a pleasure to appear before you. And thank you for everything you are doing as well.

Mr. GARRETT. Thank you.

You know, you keep stay saying stuff that makes me want to say more stuff. So I apologize.

It is so frustrating. And so earlier, I believe, the IRGC was mentioned in the context of Iran and some of, what, the four Americans currently being held by that regime, which obviously as soon as they released a certain subset of Americans found some more Americans to hold.

And it strikes me that the regime is undergirded, obviously—and we are taking about Iran, not China now, but we are on the same subject, which is global human rights—by the perpetuation of the IRGC, and specifically the Quds Force thereof. Any group of people willing to shoot their brothers and sisters in the face in the street is a difficult obstacle to overcome when you choose to exercise peaceful means of protest for expanded human rights.

But what you said that sort of struck a vein was that the Chinese are not going to turn their backs and walk away from us because they are frustrated that we have discussed human rights. So, too, I would argue that if you remove the money that supports the IRGC, which supports the Quds subset thereof, and arguably Hezbollah globally, that you will see a climate wherein things like the Green Revolution are more likely to be successful.

And so I will take this opportunity to chide the nameless masses who are more concerned with losing money by virtue of the termination of trade relationships with entities like the IRGC, or in some instances even China, than they are with people who have done more to perpetuate human rights and individual dignity and honor than they ever will, that if we stood up with a unified voice and said to the world, you can do business with the United States of America or the IRGC, for example, that the world would choose to do business with the United States of America. And millions of good Iranian people who yearn to have self-determination and freedom and wish to exercise tolerance toward their brothers and sisters could be the leaders therein.

So keep doing what you are doing. I think the reason there is no more hue and cry, candidly, is because folks like Chris Smith, who have been at this for years, folks like Frank Wolf, who is somebody I genuinely admire, were unable to get the message to a broad enough subset. But there is nothing in Washington, DC, that I can find that transcends political partisanship like the concept that every human being is entitled to a basic level of dignity and self-determination.

And I think we can do things. I really do. But I think we need to make hard choices and say, you know what, this revenue today, this money today, this business opportunity today will be there tomorrow, but right now we need to say no because there are greater things at stake.

So I thank you all for what you do. It is an honor to sit here next to you. And, hopefully, we can get more people aware of circumstances like these. Because I think without ever dropping a bomb or firing a gun we can bring change that frees human beings who have an inherent, God-given, in my opinion, right, to self-determination and freedom.

Thank you immensely, and I look forward to working with you all in the future.

Thank you, Chairman Smith.

Mr. SMITH. Thank you so very much, Mr. Garrett, for your very eloquent summation and your questioning.

Let me just, if I could, ask you all to join me in a moment of prayerful silence for Liu Xiaobo.

[Moment of silence observed.]

Mr. SMITH. The hearing is adjourned.

[Whereupon, at 12:39 p.m., the subcommittee was adjourned.]

A P P E N D I X

MATERIAL SUBMITTED FOR THE RECORD

SUBCOMMITTEE HEARING NOTICE
COMMITTEE ON FOREIGN AFFAIRS
U.S. HOUSE OF REPRESENTATIVES
WASHINGTON, DC 20515-6128

Subcommittee on Africa, Global Health, Global Human Rights, and International Organizations
Christopher H. Smith (R-NJ), Chairman

July 14, 2017

TO: MEMBERS OF THE COMMITTEE ON FOREIGN AFFAIRS

You are respectfully requested to attend an OPEN hearing of the Committee on Foreign Affairs, to be held by the Subcommittee on Subcommittee on Africa, Global Health, Global Human Rights, and International Organizations in Room 2172 of the Rayburn House Office Building (and available live on the Committee website at http://www.ForeignAffairs.house.gov):

DATE: Friday, July 14, 2017

TIME: 10:00 a.m.

SUBJECT: The Tragic Case of Liu Xiaobo

WITNESSES: Yang Jianli, Ph.D.
                       President
                       Initiatives for China

                       Perry Link, Ph.D.
                       Chancellorial Chair for Innovative Teaching
                       University of California, Riverside

                       Mr. Jared Genser
                       Founder
                       Freedom Now

By Direction of the Chairman

COMMITTEE ON FOREIGN AFFAIRS

MINUTES OF SUBCOMMITTEE ON _Africa, Global Health, Global Human Rights, and International Organizations_ HEARING

Day: _Friday_ Date _July 14, 2017_ Room _2172 Rayburn_

Starting Time _10:00 a.m._ Ending Time _12:38 p.m._

Recesses | _1_ | (_10:49_ to _11:43_) (____ to ____) (____ to ____) (____ to ____) (____ to ____) (____ to ____)

Presiding Member(s)

Rep. Chris Smith

Check all of the following that apply:

Open Session ☑ Electronically Recorded (taped) ☑
Executive (closed) Session ☐ Stenographic Record ☑
Televised ☑

TITLE OF HEARING:

The Tragic Case of Liu Xiaobo

SUBCOMMITTEE MEMBERS PRESENT:

Rep. Karen Bass, Rep. Tom Suozzi, Rep. Tom Garrett

NON-SUBCOMMITTEE MEMBERS PRESENT: _(Mark with an * if they are not members of full committee.)_

Rep. Nancy Pelosi*, Rep. Ed Royce

HEARING WITNESSES: Same as meeting notice attached? Yes ☑ No ☐
(If "no", please list below and include title, agency, department, or organization.)

STATEMENTS FOR THE RECORD: _(List any statements submitted for the record.)_

TIME SCHEDULED TO RECONVENE __________
or
TIME ADJOURNED _12:38 p.m._

Subcommittee Staff Associate